5-MINUTE BALANCE

— EXERCISES —

SENIORS

The Illustrated Guide to Fall Prevention with Simple Home Exercises to Improve Balance and Posture & Never Fear Falling Again + 30-day Workout Plan!

ALFRED ALLEN

HOME WORKOUTS FOR SENIORS OVER 60

TABLE OF CONTENTS

INTRODUCTION

Growing older is a normal part of life, and there is a lot to learn about how to do it well. Even if you have been healthy your entire life, old age can put a damper on your overall sense of well-being. As you begin to age, your body changes and slows down. You may experience stiff joints, loss of balance, and loss of bone density, among other issues.

Losing your balance is one of the most common issues in older age, and most of the time it is related to your inner ear. The vestibular system, located within your ear, is what allows you to orient yourself within space and balance your body as you move around. As you age, there is some natural decline within this system, which is why exercising, eating properly, and taking care of yourself are crucial to longevity.

Exercising can help you physically and mentally as you start to age. From a mental health perspective, exercise relieves anxiety and can help you feel more motivated and confident in your daily life. In terms of physical health, exercise can improve your brain function and help you strengthen your muscles and regulate your balance, which can prevent falls and injuries. Continuing to exercise—or starting to if you haven't exercised much in your younger years—can also prevent the onset of certain diseases and mitigate the effects of others.

If balance is something you haven't struggled with before, it can feel quite debilitating when you begin to experience accidents and injuries doing everyday tasks, such as working, golfing, grocery shopping, gardening, going for walks, and cleaning. Because the body and mind are so interconnected, seemingly minor physical ailments can directly impact your ability to maintain your independence, and therefore, your psychological well-being. This is why balance training is so very beneficial. Balance training is a subset of exercises that strengthens muscles in your legs and torso that keep you upright.

The best part about balance training is that anyone can take part in it, regardless of age or current fitness level. It can be simple and forgiving, involving small motions that aren't too physically taxing. As your fitness and balance improve, you can increase the difficulty of the exercises so they grow with you. For example, you can start small by holding basic poses. There is also some basic equipment you can use to stabilize yourself such as blocks, rolled-up blankets, weights, or rubber exercise bands. Once you feel comfortable holding a few yoga poses, you can start to ramp up your exercises to challenge your elasticity and strength, which will contribute to improved flexibility, mobility, and stability.

Over time, your balance will improve—especially if you continue to add more challenging movements to your exercises. Balance exercises can be done at any time of day or night and for however long you decide. You can practice every day, or even multiple times a day; just make sure to listen to your body and not take on more than it can handle. It is also recommended to have a workout plan in place, which is why we provide a 21-day routine at the end of the book.

After you complete the 21-day routine, you'll repeat it, adding new exercises as you feel led so you can learn to be consistent and develop healthy habits. Write down each exercise that you plan to do each day and schedule a time when you will typically do them. This will help you stay on top of things and can inspire you to work out.

Aging is inevitable so we might as well do it right and celebrate! This book will teach you why exercise is so important for anyone aging. It will cover the causes and symptoms of loss of balance, what to do if you start to experience symptoms, and how to prevent falling. You will also learn about some natural remedies you can use for balance and dizziness.

Awareness is the first step in helping you improve your lifestyle, regardless of your age. If you spend a little time and energy reading this book and trying out some new practices, you will see incredible results—increased balance and mobility, better sleep, more motivation, and confidence. Why not try? You're worth it!

CHAPTER 1
Causes and Symptoms of Balance Loss

Symptoms of Balance Loss

The causes and symptoms of balance loss can differ from person to person; everyone's bodies are different, and certain things may affect you more than others. Your body has many systems and moving parts that need to function well in order to keep your balance upright. These include the skeletal, muscular, circulatory, and nervous systems, in addition to your vision and the vestibular system in your inner ear. If something is awry, you will start to feel dizzy and sick.

Before we explore specific conditions that cause balance loss, let's talk about what it might feel like to experience symptoms of balance loss. Understanding symptoms will make it easier to talk to your family and doctors about what's going on. If you start to experience any of these symptoms, it is best to call your doctor and schedule an appointment. If you dismiss your symptoms, your balance problems can worsen, which can make them more difficult to treat.

Some symptoms you may feel when suffering from balance loss include the following:

- feeling lightheaded
- feeling dizzy
- experiencing the room spin
- loss of stability when walking, feeling like you will fall
- stumbling, falling
- confusion
- blurred vision
- pains, aches, or ringing in your ear(s)
- weakness in your body
- pain or inflammation

Knowing and understanding your symptoms can help you sort out the underlying issues and act appropriately. Being able to share specifics about your symptoms with your doctor will help them diagnose and treat you. Make sure to tell them every detail about your balance loss, as they need to find out what the problem is so they can develop helpful treatment plans and get you back on your feet.

What to Do if You Start Experiencing Symptoms

When you start to experience symptoms of balance loss, it can be scary. If the symptoms are mild and intermittent, your first thought might be to dismiss them because they are "not that bad" or manageable. Do not wait to tell your doctor until they become severe—it doesn't help you or them!

If your symptoms are debilitating at the onset, you will probably feel some anxiety as your mind races and you think about the worst outcomes. The best thing you can do is to visit a doctor. They will be able to run the proper tests and figure out the best treatment options for you. Family physicians can also refer you to specialists such as an Ear Nose and Throat (ENT) doctor or a neurologist, who are often better versed at diagnosing and treating the specific symptoms you are experiencing.

When you visit your family doctor, bring a detailed description of what is wrong—when you get dizzy, what you think the cause could be, and what you've tried to do to control it. Come prepared with questions and do not hesitate to ask. If you are unsure of what questions to ask, think about your balance and when it is good and when it is bad. Ask yourself these questions to get a grasp of how you may be feeling.

- Do I feel nauseous?
- Am I dizzy or lightheaded?
- Is it better or worse when I sit, stand, lie down, or walk?
- Is my vision blurry?
- Does the room spin while I am lying down?
- Does my dizziness occur at specific times of day or night or during certain activities?
- When was the last time I ate and drank and what did I consume?
- Do I feel hot or cold when it happens?
- Do I have a headache or notice any sensations in my ear(s)?

These may also be some of the questions the doctor asks you to better understand your symptoms, so thinking about them ahead of time will help you be prepared and more decisive about your responses.

Many treatments are effective, but some people do have to learn to live with balance disorders. Some people seek out physical therapy (PT) to cope because there are trainers who specialize in treating vertigo and can help you gain strength to reduce your risk of falling. Ask your doctor if they think PT might be beneficial for you. One of the benefits is that physical therapists will often give you exercises to do at home so you can reap the benefits even after you stop seeing them.

Causes of Balance Loss

Now that we have a better understanding of the symptoms you might face, let's talk about what might be happening inside your body. Causes of balance loss may be attributed to something as simple as temporarily low blood sugar, which can be remedied fairly quickly with a snack or a meal, or they can be related to conditions that are not commonly known and require more intensive treatments. Let's take a closer look at some of these conditions.

Benign Paroxysmal Positional Vertigo: BPPV is a very common reason for loss of balance. It is caused by calcium crystals in your inner ear that become dislodged and move around in the spaces within your ear that are filled with fluid. When you have BPPV, you will experience a spinning sensation from the simplest eye or head movements. Other symptoms can include dizziness, nausea, and vomiting.

Vestibular neuritis: This is another common balance disorder that affects adults and elderly people. It is caused when a nerve in the inner ear becomes swollen, which causes the brain to misinterpret the information received and makes you feel dizzy. These symptoms can last anywhere from a few hours up to a few weeks.

Persistent Postural Perceptual Dizziness: PPPD is a chronic condition that is usually brought on after an inciting vertigo-inducing event such as a panic attack, a mild traumatic brain injury, a vestibular migraine, or BPPV. Most people experience symptoms—dizziness and unsteadiness that worsen when walking—daily or for more than 15 days each month. Symptoms will worsen when you are in a high-traffic area like a shopping mall.

Ménière's disease: This is a disorder of the inner ear that causes recurring episodes of vertigo. Symptoms may start with a ringing or feeling of fullness in your ear. Without treatment, you may even lose your hearing. Ménière's disease is very rare and usually happens to people between the ages of 20 to 40, but it is still something to be aware of as it's better if diagnosed and treated early on.

Migraines: The symptoms of migraines are similar to vestibular neuritis, as they can make you feel a sense of motion sickness and dizziness. This is a common issue among adults and is usually accompanied by severe headaches, sensitivity to bright light and harsh sounds, and nausea. Migraines can be treated with medication to varying degrees of success, but even so, episodes can be disruptive to daily life. Talk to your doctor about treatment options.

Low blood pressure: If you have low blood pressure, one of the most common symptoms is experiencing lightheadedness or dizziness when you stand up quickly. Blood pressure interacts with your hearing and balance.

Low blood sugar: Chronically low blood glucose levels (hypoglycemia) can cause shakiness, dizziness, and sweating. Diabetes is a very common cause of low blood sugar, which can lead to balance loss. It happens to many elderly individuals, but it can be controlled with insulin or by eating a sugary snack.

Dehydration: As we age, we tend to drink less and we are more prone to dehydration—especially if we are experiencing or recovering from an illness or surgery. One of the symptoms of not having enough fluid in our bodies is feeling lightheaded or dizzy. If not treated, symptoms can become more severe and even cause death, but luckily, treating dehydration with fluids—oral or intravenous—is simple and symptoms generally clear up quickly.

Poor circulation: This is a common condition in people who are aging. Blood vessels narrow and don't accommodate as much blood flow, which impacts oxygen delivery throughout your body. It may affect your ability to do daily tasks due to muscle pain or weakness, numbness, swelling, dizziness, and loss of balance. Poor circulation can be caused or exacerbated by smoking, high blood pressure, diabetes, blood clots, varicose veins, obesity, and cardiovascular disease.

Cardiovascular disease: This is an umbrella term for a subset of diseases that affect the blood vessels and heart and; it is the leading cause of death worldwide. Your heart pumps blood and oxygen, and your arteries and veins deliver it to your brain and throughout your entire body. If the heart muscle or valves become damaged, or if the blood vessels become blocked, the most common result is heart failure, stroke, or cardiac arrest. Those living with cardiovascular disease may experience dizziness or loss of balance.

Iron deficiency: When your red blood cells aren't getting enough iron, it prevents them from producing hemoglobin, which is what allows them to carry and deliver oxygen to and throughout your body. Symptoms of low iron levels include fatigue, weakness, headaches, lightheadedness, and dizziness, in addition to feeling cold and looking pale. Eating iron-rich foods and taking supplements regularly help restore your iron levels and make you feel better.

Joint, vision, or muscle problems: Unsteady joints or weak muscles can cause you to lose your balance, especially as you age. Untreated vision problems can also lead to dizziness. Many of these issues can be managed with proper treatment.

Parkinson's disease: This is a brain disorder that affects the central nervous system; it inhibits your brain from releasing necessary chemicals into your body. The loss of dopamine causes issues with movement, and the loss of norepinephrine makes it hard for your body to elevate your blood pressure, leaving you feeling lightheaded. As Parkinson's progresses, muscles stiffen and become rigid, changing your gait and making it difficult to get around. There is no known cure as of yet, so doctors try to treat symptoms as best they can. Balance exercises are critical for people living with Parkinson's.

Side effects of certain medicines: If you are experiencing dizziness after starting a new medication or temporarily taking over-the-counter medication, one of the side effects of that drug may be issues with balance such as dizziness, lightheadedness, or nausea. Talk it over with your doctor to see if there are other medications to try instead, or if there are ways to manage the symptoms if you do have to stay on the medication.

As you can see, there are many causes of losing your balance so it's helpful to understand them as you age. First, we identify and document symptoms, then we can visit our doctors, speculate about what might be going on, and with their help, try to prevent or mitigate further symptoms when possible. In the next chapter, we'll take a look at how doctors can begin to properly diagnose what's going on. Knowledge is power—especially in our current healthcare system—so arm yourself with all that you can so you can be your best advocate.

CHAPTER 2
How to Diagnose and Treat Balance Loss

Tests to Diagnose Balance Loss

Because balance loss can have multiple causes, treating it can be difficult when you don't know why it's happening. Doctors will often run multiple tests to rule out causes and diagnose the issue. The most common tests they might run include the following.

Hearing tests: Audiologists conduct hearing tests for many different reasons. Most of the time, you will be asked to put on headphones, listen for different sounds, and signal when you hear them by raising a hand. Hearing tests measure volume (in decibels) and frequency or pitch (in Hertz) to determine whether there is any hearing loss and how significant it is. As people age, it's common to lose some hearing in the high frequencies, but hearing loss is complex and unique to each person. When your symptoms are dizziness and nausea, for example, you might not even notice hearing loss, but it can all be interrelated.

Balance tests: Balance tests can help diagnose why you are feeling a certain way and what might be causing it. The series of tests generally conducted is called electronystagmography (ENG) or videonystagmography (VNG)—they assess your eyes, inner ears, and parts of your brain. To do this test, the doctor (audiologist, otolaryngologist, or neurologist) will place electrodes above your eyes (ENG) or goggles with two infrared cameras over both of your eyes (VNG) and direct you to do a series of things as the electrodes or cameras record your eye movement. In addition to standing, you may also be asked to lie down. One portion of the test may include introducing warm water or cool air into your ear to gauge the reaction in your eyes. The tests take about an hour and help doctors determine the root cause of your balance issues.

Vision and eye movement tests: These tests are very important when it comes to dizziness, as your eyes can affect your balance and hand-eye coordination. Eye movement tests will help assess weaknesses in your vision and eye muscles. They may find that you have uncontrolled movements of the eye, double vision, or blurry vision—near or far. Having good ocular movement is beneficial for improving your memory, focus, and vision all in one. If your eyes are a contributing issue to your balance loss, you may have to start wearing glasses, or even undergo eye surgery.

MRI scan: An MRI scan allows specific parts of your body to be fully scanned so the doctors can get a structural picture. It presents the doctors with clear and detailed images of whatever is being scanned—brain, legs, stomach, and even bones or joints—to diagnose issues and identify potential problem areas so they can recommend next steps and referrals to specialists.

Blood pressure test: A nurse or doctor in your medical practice will check your blood pressure each time you visit to make sure it is within normal limits. The most typical blood pressure test is administered with a stethoscope and pressure cuff (or sphygmomanometer) and it measures pressure in your arteries when your heart is contracting (systolic) and relaxed (diastolic). Having consistently low blood pressure (hypotension) can cause dizziness, lightheadedness, fainting, fatigue, nausea, and vision problems. You may not experience symptoms if you have high blood pressure (hypertension), but it can lead to stroke, heart attack, or heart failure if not detected and treated.

Heart rate test: Your pulse is an important indicator of your heart health, which is why nurses and doctors always measure it. According to Healthline, "Your age and fitness level have a big impact on your resting heart rate," which should be between 60 and 100 beats per minute (Dix, 2019). If your heart rate is too fast or too slow; it can cause balance loss and nausea, making it difficult to do daily tasks. Be sure to get your heart checked regularly.

Posturography tests: These tests evaluate your balance while you are standing. The doctor will have you stand barefoot on the ground while wearing a harness. There will be a screen around you showing certain landscapes that change. The platform you are standing on will start to move. You may repeat the test with your eyes closed. This test allows doctors to quantify the results of your balance and measure it over time.

CT scan: This test is similar to an MRI, but CT scans use advanced X-ray technology. CT scans are often used before and after surgical procedures and are useful when you have heart disease, cancer, or even a concussion. They can also help doctors be aware of issues such as blood clots or internal bleeding.

Video head impulse test: The VHIT is an ear test that looks for disorders affecting vestibular dysfunction in the inner ear. You wear lightweight goggles that capture eye movement and send information to a computer as the doctor will slightly turn your head in different directions.

When you go in for balance tests, make sure you are wearing comfortable, loose-fitting clothing. Consult with your doctor so you know how to prepare before your appointment. Depending on the test, you may need to restrict what you eat or drink, or the medication you take. You may also be asked to refrain from exercise for a certain number of hours or days leading up to the tests. For tests involving your eyes, be sure to ask about wearing contact lenses or glasses.

Ways to Treat Balance Loss

The tests doctors perform will either point to a conclusive diagnosis and treatment plan or come back with normal results. If the latter happens, your doctor may pursue other avenues of investigation. In the meantime, you can still be proactive in dealing with your symptoms. Here are five ways to mitigate balance loss.

Balance exercises: These are the most typical way to regain balance because they help you regain strength in your muscles. Consult a physical therapist to guide you as they will be the most knowledgeable. They may suggest an assistive device to walk with, such as a cane, to improve balance over time.

Diet changes: Changes in your diet can help with balance, especially when you suffer from headaches. Lean protein, for example, will help your ability and endurance to stand and balance yourself every day. Avoiding alcohol, caffeine, and junk food will also help your symptoms and lead to a healthier lifestyle.

Positioning routines: These are good techniques to do if you struggle with inner ear conditions. They move your head in different positions to move particles from one part of your ear to another. Treatments to look into include: the Canalith repositioning procedure, the Epley maneuver, Semont maneuver, Half-somersault or Foster maneuver, and the Brandt-Daroff Exercise. You may be able to perform some of these yourself at home, but consult your doctor or therapist first.

Medications: Doctors may prescribe medications if lifestyle changes won't be enough. If you have bad vertigo that causes vomiting that lasts multiple days, you will probably be prescribed medication to control your dizziness and nausea in the interim.

Surgery: If your vertigo is severe enough, you may need surgery. This is more common in patients that have Ménière's disease or acoustic neuroma—a benign tumor that develops on the nerves going from your inner ear to the brain.

Because balance loss can have multiple causes and require overlapping treatment, it's always best to try to coordinate your care across the various doctors, specialists, and therapists you might see so that information and results are shared by your care team and you get the best care and results you can.

Ways to Prevent Falls

You can also do things at home or out and about to prevent falls. Some might seem obvious, but it never hurts to mention them because the majority of falls are preventable. (And people who suffer from a preventable fall often want to kick themselves for not being more careful with something obvious!)

Handrails

- *Stairs:* Use handrails while walking up and down stairs. Because our minds are usually on autopilot going up or down the stairs, and it's a terrible place to fall, stairs can be quite dangerous. It's always best to have something to hold onto to stabilize yourself.

- *Bathroom:* Install and use a system of handles to assist you when you get in and out of the bathtub or shower, and on and off the toilet. Consider using a bath mat with grips for the floor of the tub or shower.

Trip hazards

- *Items:* Remove items from the floor at home, so there is no way you can trip and fall on your own belongings.

- *Rugs:* Secure area rugs with a rubber backing and/or tape so they don't move when you step on them. Pay special attention to corners or edges that may cause tripping hazards.

Surfaces

- Do your best to avoid water on slippery surfaces and ice outside.

- Take notice of surface changes (material and depth) while walking indoors and outdoors.

Shoes: Wear flat shoes with good tread—especially on smooth surfaces such as tile or wood floors.

Assistive devices: If your doctor has recommended you use an assistive device (ankle/knee brace, cane, crutch, walker, or scooter), do it. They recommended it so that you would be safer and more confident in your abilities.

Night lights: Plug in night lights around your house so you don't walk around in the dark. This one gets people of any age!

Rise slowly: Get up slowly, especially from a prone to standing position. Stay seated for a few moments before you stand to allow your body to regulate the flow of blood and oxygen.

Alcohol: Limit your alcohol consumption so you don't exacerbate existing balance problems.

The tips above together with maintaining a healthy weight, keeping your muscles limber with regular exercise, checking on and treating any bone density issues, and scheduling regular doctor check-ups will help prevent falls and the negative mental and physical effects that accompany them.

CHAPTER 3
Natural Remedies for Balance Loss

In addition to a healthy diet and adequate water intake, natural remedies are an amazing way to start living healthier. They generally cost less money than traditional medicines and treatments, and most don't require you to leave the house. Remedies include vitamin and herbal supplements, certain foods, and exercises you can try to combat your balance issues. As you read through, make a note of which ones you'd like to research further.

Homeopathy

Homeopathy is a holistic approach to wellness that is predicated on believing that the body can cure itself. While its effectiveness is challenged by the traditional medical community, many people swear by its natural remedies, which are derived from herbs, minerals, or animal products. Practitioners, called homeopaths, treat each person according to their specific body makeup and symptoms, which means that people reporting the same symptoms may be given different treatments. The National Center for Complementary and Integrative Health provides a few helpful suggestions for combining homeopathic treatments with traditional medicine (2022):

- Don't use homeopathy to replace proven conventional care or postpone seeing a health care provider about a medical problem.
- If you are considering using a homeopathic product, bring it with you when you visit your healthcare provider. The provider may be able to help you determine whether the product might pose a risk of side effects or drug interactions.
- Take charge of your health—talk with your health care providers about any complementary health approaches you use. Together, you can make shared, well-informed decisions.

There are three types of natural remedies we'll discuss: Vitamin supplements, food and drink, and herbs and oils. Each one has healing properties and can help you manage and treat your balance loss.

Vitamin Supplements

Vitamins are important in order to become healthy and strong, and in a perfect world, we would get all our required vitamins and minerals from the foods we eat. Because we know that doesn't happen on a regular basis, the next best thing we can do is supplement our diets with vitamins—especially in those areas we may have deficiencies. For example, seniors may take calcium and fish oil to protect their bones and heart. When suffering from balance loss, it is crucial to take vitamins every day to be able to manage symptoms of dizziness. Here are the most common vitamins doctors suggest taking for balance loss.

Vitamin C: This vitamin can help relieve symptoms of dizziness that are associated with Ménière's disease and vertigo. It is not a permanent fix, but it can temporarily work if you are consistent in taking vitamin C.

Vitamin E: This vitamin will control circulation in your body, just like vitamin D will. It helps to lessen symptoms of vertigo, headaches, lightheadedness, and blurry vision.

Vitamin D: This vitamin can help you while struggling with BPPV on a daily basis. It helps oxygen and blood flow through your body, which can reduce symptoms of dizziness and lightheadedness.

Calcium: There is a new study out that calcium can help symptoms of dizziness. Doctors recommend you take calcium twice a day to relieve dizziness and pain. It's a low-risk way to help symptoms, as well as build your calcium intake. The study took 850 patients who suffer from balance loss, and they split them into two groups. One group took vitamin D twice a day for one year, and the other group took calcium twice a day for one year. Eighty-six percent of patients said that calcium relieved their symptoms more than vitamin D supplements did (*Vitamin D, calcium supplementation*, 2022).

Vitamin B12: Not getting enough B12 can cause balance problems in elderly people as B12 helps red blood cells form, which deliver oxygen and encourage healthy nerve function and cell metabolism. Vitamin B12 comes from great food sources, such as meat, fish, and eggs.

Food & Drink

First, start watching what you are eating and how much water you drink throughout the day—a poor diet and lack of hydration worsen balance symptoms. Dehydration is one of the many reasons older people suffer from dizziness. Ensure you have enough water intake and whole foods in your diet, especially when you struggle with balance loss symptoms. Whole foods include minimally processed or unprocessed foods, such as fruits, vegetables, and legumes, among many others. Here are suggestions for food and drink ideas to combat symptoms of balance loss.

Ginger: Ginger can help when you feel motion sickness—the ginger root has properties in it that can ease feelings of lightheadedness, dizziness, and nausea. Drinking ginger tea is a good way for your body to ingest and process it. To make ginger tea, you will want to steep the ginger root for about five minutes in a cup of hot water. Drink it twice a day to maximize the benefits.

Almonds: These are rich in nutrients and provide you with vitamins A, B, and E. Almonds also supply you with healthy fats and proteins, which can help you with symptoms of vertigo, as well as proper brain function.

Electrolytes: Electrolytes help your body stay hydrated and maintain balance—especially related to levels of sodium, magnesium, potassium, calcium, chloride, bicarbonate, and phosphate, which are very important when you're ill or exercising. According to the Cleveland Clinic, electrolytes "help your body regulate chemical reactions, maintain the balance between fluids inside and outside your cells, and more." This is important because "your cells use electrolytes to conduct electrical charges, which is how your muscles contract" (n.d.). You can add powdered electrolytes to water to reap the benefits.

Herbs & Oils

Herbs and essential oils are a great remedy to reduce symptoms of dizziness and nausea. Essential oils are completely natural, made from "leaves, seeds, barks, roots, and rinds" (WebMD, 2021). They were used well before modern medicine and still are used in this generation. There are a few main herbs and oils to use when it comes to balance loss.

Essential Oils: Certain oils can reduce signs of dizziness, headaches, and nausea. You don't need to use a delivery device to enjoy essential oils—"you can add them to vegetable oils, creams, or bath gels" (*Essential oils*, 2021) or apply them directly to your chest, the temples of your head, and neck—adding oils to these places on your body will temporarily relieve vertigo symptoms. Specific oils that can be beneficial for balance loss include lavender, ginger, peppermint, and lemon. If you have doubts about using them, ask your doctor.

Ginkgo Biloba: This is an herb originally from China that is beneficial for easing symptoms of dizziness. It has properties of the medication betahistine in it to control your vertigo and helps your blood flow from your brain through your body.

Turmeric, Cayenne, and **Lemon Balm:** All of these herbs can be taken in capsule form and act as good antioxidants and anti-inflammatories, which can help ease vertigo symptoms.

These natural home remedies are a temporary relief for dizziness and issues related to balance loss. They won't cure you, but they can help you manage symptoms. Each person will respond differently to homeopathic remedies, but in general, these vitamins, herbs, oils, and foods can help you tremendously. In conjunction with your doctor, be sure to find out what works for you.

CHAPTER 4
The Importance of Exercise

Exercise is crucial to a healthy lifestyle, longevity, and good quality of life. The most basic questions about exercise might be (1) *What constitutes physical activity?* and (2) *How much activity is recommended for older people?*

For answers to these questions, we'll lean heavily on a 2018 journal article from *BioMed Research International* that defines Physical Activity (PA), exercise, and physical function:

- **PA** is defined as any bodily movement produced by skeletal muscles that result in energy expenditure. PA encompasses exercise, sports, and physical activities performed as part of daily living, occupation, leisure, or active transportation.
- **Exercise** is a subcategory of PA that is planned, structured, and repetitive and that has as a final or intermediate objective for improvement or maintenance of physical fitness.
- **Physical function** is the capacity of an individual to perform the physical activities of daily living. Physical function reflects motor function and control, physical fitness, and habitual PA. To attain a high level of cardiorespiratory fitness, it is recommended to be physically active for six months or longer. (Langhammer et al.)

According to the World Health Institute, it's recommended that seniors be active for 150 minutes per week (2.5 hours) in addition to their daily activities, and that activity should include "aerobic exercise and strength exercise as well as balance exercises to reduce the risk of falls" (Langhammer et al., 2018). The question naturally arises, what something prevents me from doing that? The answer is: "If older adults cannot follow the guidelines because of chronic conditions, they should be as active as their ability and conditions allow" (Langhammer et al., 2018).

There are a few exercise techniques you can do daily to enhance your balance. These include yoga, neck exercises, and stretching. They are all fairly simple to do and can keep you in healthy physical condition when done regularly. Yoga stretches and strengthens, which helps your balance to become sturdier. Holding one position for a certain period of time can clear your symptoms of dizziness temporarily. Neck exercises and stretching are rather similar, as they both involve extending your body in different ways to target certain muscle groups. Neck exercises in particular work to strengthen the muscles supporting your head to help with balance.

Any kind of movement is good for you and your body as it involves physical activity. You can choose any exercise technique that suits you best—swimming, dancing, running, cardio, weights, walking—noting the recommendations above.

Benefits of Exercise

Another basic question you might be asking yourself is: *What can exercise do for me?* The short answer is that exercise provides many benefits that help with your physical and mental health. Let's look at a few of the most important benefits.

Elevated mood: Exercising can boost your mood and allow you to release unwanted emotions. Happiness is the key to living a healthy life, as it can make you feel more positive and reduce feelings of pain. Exercising provides you with a boost of motivation and energy, which we can all use regardless of our age.

Weight loss: Moving your body can reduce weight from the calories you burn.

Although, if this is your goal, you cannot expect your body to lose weight overnight—it takes time, effort, and consistency. The best exercises you can do for weight loss include cardio and walking, however, you should be aware of your diet while exercising too. If you lose too much weight, it can be unhealthy. Make sure you are eating lots of fruits and veggies, as well as whole foods, which are minimally processed or unprocessed foods. You will also want to ensure you are getting enough water too.

Stronger muscles and bones: Exercising can help you gain stronger muscles. As you age, your muscles and bones tend to weaken, which can become a daily problem for you. Some exercises that may help include: Lifting weights, squats, lunges, push-ups, resistance machines, and resistance bands. Strength training can also improve your coordination, balance, and ability to move properly.

Increased energy: Energy allows you to have the ability to do tasks throughout the day. Exercising regularly helps to keep your oxygen circulating through your body, which boosts your energy. Not only does it increase your mood, but it can also help your body move better.

Reduced risk of chronic disease: Exercising can relieve symptoms of chronic diseases, as it can provide you with better heart health, cholesterol levels, and blood pressure, among other benefits. Exercise can help you reduce symptoms of type 2 diabetes, cancer, heart disease, hypertension, and high cholesterol. It is recommended that people with these diseases exercise regularly, or even daily, to prevent the diseases and their symptoms from worsening.

Better skin health: Exercising can improve your overall skin, as it can help reduce stress and tension in your body. Your body has antioxidant defenses related to oxidant stress which sometimes cannot repair the cell damage done-this can cause serious damage to your skin. Although, exercise can help release antioxidants to protect your cells from more damage. This is specifically important when you are aging, as exercise can make your skin look brighter and younger again.

Improved memory and brain health: Exercising keeps your brain running smoothly and helps you reduce memory loss so that you remember important information and long-term memories. Regular exercise is important in elderly people as it can improve inflammation, oxidative stress, and brain structure. This can be helpful with patients who suffer from Alzheimer's and dementia.

Reduced pain: Exercise can increase levels of serotonin which can reduce pain and inflammation in your body. Moving your body can loosen up your muscles, bones, and joints to control swelling and bruising in specific spots of your skin. This is particularly great when you start to age because your muscles start to weaken; practicing exercises can help to replenish them.

Better sleep quality: Exercise can give you motivation throughout the day to be able to burn energy, so you can sleep properly. Even exercises before bed can give you a good quality of sleep. When you move your body in the evening, it allows you to relax and become more tired—this can improve the quality of sleep you will get through the night. Not only that, but exercise also raises your body temperature. If you do a few exercises for half an hour or so before bed, your temperature will fall, allowing you to fall asleep more peacefully.

The final question we focus on briefly is: *What do I risk if I don't exercise as a senior?* We can easily go back through the list above and negate the positives, but that may not speak to the scale of the problem. Inactivity in seniors is high—one in every four to five adults is physically inactive, or is less active than the WHO recommends—and the risks are substantial. For details, we'll once again lean on authors Langhammer, Bergland, and Rydwik.

"Inactivity and aging increase the risk of chronic disease, and older people often have multiple chronic conditions" (2018). Inactivity is correlated with changes in our body composition that results in a higher percentage of body fat and a reduction in lean body mass. Muscles atrophy when not used. Inactive seniors risk falls and debilitating injuries with slow and incomplete recoveries. We become at higher risk for "noncommunicable diseases such as cardiovascular disease, stroke, diabetes, and some types of cancer... A lack of physical activity also negatively impacts our mental health, and can contribute to poor executive control and an earlier onset of dementia" (2018).

Tips for Exercise

When it comes to exercising, there are some basic tips to employ that will help you along your balance and fitness journey. The tips all have to do with being prepared and mindful before, during, and after your workout to boost your energy, increase your motivation, and reduce your risk of injuries.

Drinking water is one of the best things you can do while working out—it keeps you hydrated, and helps you perform exercises efficiently. You should drink water before, during, and after your workout routine—try to drink at least eight glasses of water each day.

Eating: Before your workout, you'll want to ensure that you eat a nutritious meal for energy and muscle function. Having a small nutritional snack available during your workout is another good option, just be sure to keep intake to a minimum during a workout so you don't experience stomach cramps.

Rest: During your workouts, it is crucial to rest between each exercise. Shake out the muscles you've been working. Walk around a bit; sit if you need to. While you want to challenge yourself *during* an exercise, you don't want to overdo it by doing multiple strenuous exercises in a row without a rest period in between. Pause. Take a bite of a granola bar and a sip of water, and then continue with your workout routine.

Stretching is a very important part of your workout so that you avoid injuries and unnecessary soreness (some soreness is perfectly normal). Before you begin working out, you'll want to stretch your muscles to increase blood (and oxygen) circulation and to get them limber for what's to come. After a workout routine, you should practice some cool-down exercises. Stretching or light movement is perfect for cooldowns and will help reduce muscle soreness. The most common exercise mistakes are ignoring the warmup and cooldown.

Keeping cool: If you plan to exercise outside, be sure the sun exposure, temperature, and humidity are reasonable. Consider exercising outdoors first thing in the morning or the early evening. For indoor workouts, have a fan nearby to circulate air and cool you off. Finally, after a workout, take a shower with cooler water and change out of your workout clothing.

Breathing: One of the most important things to remember while doing any kind of physical activity is to breathe. This may sound silly because breathing is involuntary, meaning we don't have to think about it. But, during exercise, it's the exact opposite. We have to be extremely mindful about when we inhale and exhale because when we don't think about it, we tend to do it wrong. Our instinct is to hold our breath and that's what gets us in trouble. Let's say you're about to lift weights. Picture yourself in front of a heavy dumbbell. Your natural reaction might be to take a breath and hold it as you "muscle through" the exercise, then exhale after you put the weight down. What if I told you that you needed to do the exact opposite?

The key to breathing during exercise is to inhale as you relax and exhale as you expend energy. Now think about doing a traditional sit-up. As you lift yourself to a seated position crunching those abdominal muscles, you are breathing out. When you start to relax and lie back down on the mat, you're inhaling, bringing air into your lungs and circulatory system. Envision yourself doing that a few times in a row. You'll probably find that it doesn't come naturally, which is fine. It just means you'll have to focus on it when exercising until, forgive the pun, it becomes as normal as breathing. AARP recommends practicing during cooldowns and stretching (lower intensity exercises) so you "get better at taking consistent and even inhales and exhales" (Theifels, 2017).

Maintaining good posture: Another common mistake to avoid is having bad posture when performing exercises as it tends to work the wrong muscles and leave you sore in places you ought not to be. If our chests aren't open and our shoulders back, we're actually restricting air flow into our lungs, which will make us more tired and out of breath. When we get tired, we tend to have sloppy form and that's when injuries can happen. For example, if you're not engaging your abdominal muscles during certain exercises, you're more likely to put undue strain on your back or neck. If your stance during a lunge is overextended, it's easy to injure your knee. Good form is really important for oxygen intake, making exercises target the correct muscles, and avoiding injury to joints and muscles. If you're attending a group fitness class or have a personal trainer or a physical therapist, be sure to listen to their instructions carefully, imitate their movements, ask for corrections, and ask questions if you're unsure about your form. Aside from listening to your own body's limits, this is the best way to learn and keep yourself safe.

In the next chapter, you will learn how to do specific balance exercises to improve your balance issues and related symptoms. The exercises you will learn about are important because each one allows you to gain flexibility and mobility, as well as reduce symptoms associated with your balance, such as dizziness or nausea. Each exercise guides you to move fluidly to lessen your risk of injuries and will promote strength in your muscles, joints, and bones, as well as improve your hand-eye coordination. All exercises take as long as five minutes to complete and can be suitable for all fitness levels—especially beginners.

CHAPTER 5
Balance Exercises for Seniors

xercise is important at any age, and as we just learned, it is very important for seniors. In this section, we will talk through 55 exercises you can do to improve your balance. They are divided into four categories: Standing, seated, lying, and walking. For each, we'll detail how to practice them, which modifications or variations you can do, and what safety precautions to be aware of. Performing an exercise in a different way can help you enjoy your workout plan more and provide you with more motivation to accomplish it. Variations are a safe way to practice exercises as they can target slightly different muscle groups or areas of your body.

PART

1

STANDING BALANCE

EXERCISES

EXERCISE 1
WEIGHT SHIFT

1.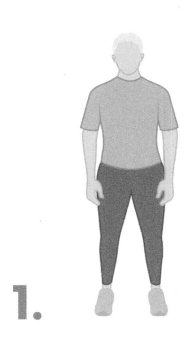

2.

Weight shifting is one of the best exercises you can do to control your balance and ease balance loss symptoms. You can practice weight shifting by balancing on one leg and then on the other. There are many benefits to weight shifting which include improving balance symptoms, strengthening lower-body muscles, and providing more coordination.

Instructions

1. Stand up as straight as you can with your feet shoulder-width apart

2. Lift your left leg fully off the ground, so all of your weight is on your right foot.

3. Hold the position for up to 20 seconds and then put your left leg down.

4. Repeat the first steps with your opposite foot.

5. Make sure to practice each side three times.

Variations: When practicing weight shifts, it is also important to learn about the possible variations.

- Eyes-closed weight shifts: Repeat the exercise above with your eyes closed.
- Forward and back weight shifts: Instead of lifting your straight leg up, point your toes and kick it forward a bit. Come back to standing and then lift that leg behind you.
- Lateral weight shift exercises: When you lift your leg, swing it out to the side and hold your balance.

EXERCISE 2
ROCK THE BOAT

1.

2.

This exercise is very similar to weight shifting.

Rock the Boat improves balance symptoms and relieves stress or tension from your body, as it promotes flexibility and provides you with more mobility to do simple tasks throughout the day. The exercise requires no equipment, except for something to support your balance if needed.

Instructions

1. Stand with your feet hip-width apart.

2. Lift your left leg sideways and hold this position for 2 seconds.

3. Return to the starting position

4. Now lift your right leg laterally and hold this position for 2 seconds.

5. Repeat the previous steps up to 10 times per leg.

EXERCISE 3
KNEE RAISING

Knee Raising is useful for improving balance, posture and strengthening the lower body.

For added safety, it is best to have a chair or other support object on the side, in case you need support while performing the exercise.

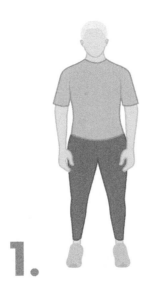

1.

2.

1. Stand up as straight as you can. Use a walker or chair to steady yourself if needed. Place your feet hip-width.

2. Extend each of your arms out to the sides of your body.

3. Keep your arms extended at your sides and lift your left foot off of the ground. Bring your knee up as high as you can in front of you.

4. Hold the pose for up to 30 seconds to gain balance. If it is too hard at first, hold the position for 20 seconds using a chair at the side for support if necessary.

5. Repeat the same steps on your right foot.

6. Repeat these steps three times on each side to provide the maximum benefit.

Variations: There are two variations of this exercise to try if you are looking for a comfortable and more secure way to practice them. They both have the same beneficial outcomes but are accomplished differently.

- The blanket method: This helps you decrease your risk of injury in your legs, stomach, and back. If you have recently undergone surgery, or if you are in recovery, this will be the best variation for you. For this method, all you need to do is lie down on the ground, place a comfortable blanket underneath where you are practicing this exercise, and pull your knee up as directed.

- The block method: This is a great one to try out as it strengthens the muscles in your arms and abdominal area. It guides you to control your balance, and dizziness symptoms. To perform this exercise, sit on the floor and extend your arms to the sides. Have two yoga blocks near you. (You can also use a step stool.) When you lift each knee up, rest each foot lightly on the yoga blocks as you are sitting on a mat on the floor.

EXERCISE 4
TREE POSE

1.

2.

3.

The tree pose exercise is a technique used in yoga. While it can be difficult at first, as it requires you to balance steadily without any support from walls or chairs, there are many benefits:

- Better sleep quality.
- fewer balance symptoms.
- strengthened muscles.
- better hand-eye coordination.

Instructions

1. Stand still with your feet spread apart.

2. Rotate your right hip outward so that your toes are pointed to the right.

3. Elevate the heel on your right foot so your toes are lightly touching the ground.

4. As you do, shift your weight to the left side of your body. Try lifting your toes (right foot) off the floor and balancing.

5. Raise your arms directly over your head with your palms facing inward and hold that stance for up to 45 seconds.

6. Repeat the first three steps with your opposite foot.

Tips: If the duration indicated below is too long, try reducing the duration and having an object by your side for support

Variation: This is a more challenging variation, with the same benefits:

- Half-lotus tree pose: Stand on one leg. Bend the knee of the other leg and bring your ankle up to rest against your thigh above your knee.

EXERCISE 5
FLAMINGO STAND

1.

2.

The flamingo is definitely the first animal that comes to mind when talking about balance. Its way of balancing on one leg will therefore be our inspiration for this exercise.

The flamingo stand exercise builds strength in your trunk, leg, and pelvic muscles to control your dizziness and helps you with symptoms of vertigo.

Instructions

1. Stand up straight with your feet hip-width apart, with a chair in front of you in case you need support.

2. Lift your left foot off the ground and bring it back.

3. Hold the position for 20 seconds, supporting yourself using your fingertips with the chair if you are about to lose your balance.

4. Return to the starting position and perform the exercise with your right leg.

5. Repeat the exercise 3 times per leg

EXERCISE 6
WALL PUSH-UPS

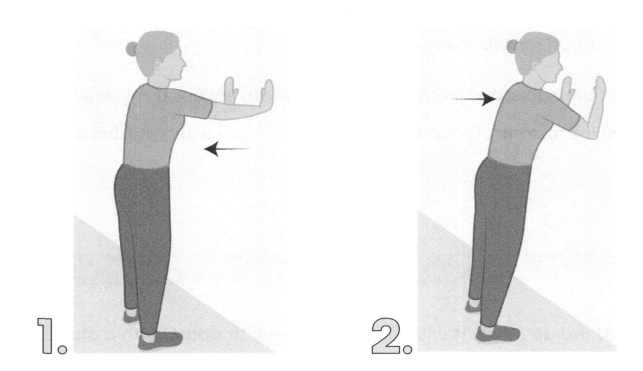

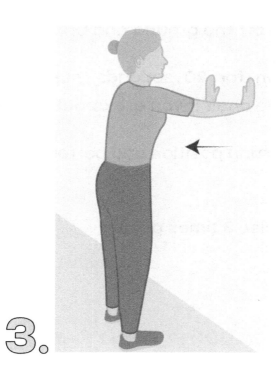

This exercise is great to increase your stability and mobility. Wall push-ups strengthen muscles in your arms, shoulders, and chest, which can help you remain stable while standing and walking. While wall push-ups are beneficial for your balance, they should **only be practiced once a week or less.** If you do this exercise every day, you may experience soreness and wrist pain, elbow pain, and lower back pain.

Instructions

1. Stand with your arms shoulder-width apart in front of you. Extend them fully so that they are touching a wall. Make sure your palms are flat on the wall and at the same height as your shoulders.
2. Keep both feet flat on the ground and slightly lean toward the wall.
3. Push yourself back and forth, just like you are doing push-ups on the ground.
4. Do up to 20 repetitions.

Variations: There are three variations for wall push-ups that can suit your fitness level—whether you are a beginner or more advanced. Some of these variations are more difficult than others, but you can choose those you feel most comfortable with.

- Close hands wall push-ups: Bring your hands closer together during push-ups.
- One arm wall push-ups: Try the exercise using only one arm to push up with.
- One leg wall push-ups: Try lifting a leg at the knee out behind you during a push-up.

EXERCISE 7
BACK LEG RAISES

1.

2.

Back leg raises help you gain strength in your back, glutes, and legs, which benefits for your posture. Leg exercises also create firmness in your abdominal muscles.

Instructions

1. Place your hands on your walker, chair, or even a wall. Put all of your weight on the right side of your body.

2. Lift your left leg up and backward as high as you possibly can.

3. Hold your leg in the air for five seconds.

4. Put your leg down and keep your hands on the object you are using to balance yourself.

5. Do these steps 10 more times on the same leg.

6. Repeat all the steps on the other leg.

EXERCISE 8
FOOT TAP STEPS

This exercise is perfect for those experiencing a loss of balance. It allows you to improve your balance and coordination. It also helps you when you are walking up and down stairs.

1.

2.

Instructions

To do this exercise properly, you need to be near a staircase or use a step stool.

1. Stand up straight in front of the step stool or staircase.

2. Lift your right foot onto the first step, then place it back down beside your left foot.

3. Take the left foot and place it on the step, then back down onto the ground.

4. Repeat these steps. For the best outcome, you should repeat 10 repetitions, two to three times on each leg.

Variations: There are a few variations to try out that can reduce the monotony in this particular exercise.

- Seated toe taps: Follow the same steps above, but in a seated position.
- Higher platform toe taps: Using a higher platform to lift your leg onto makes this exercise more challenging.
- Loaded toe taps: Consider using ankle weights to increase the difficulty of the exercise.
- Increased speed toe taps: Try timing yourself and counting how many toe taps you can complete in 30 seconds. Then you can beat your record.
- Shorter platform toe taps: If a stair or step stool is too challenging initially, tap on the ground or a lower platform until you feel more confident.

EXERCISE 9
SIDE LEG RAISES

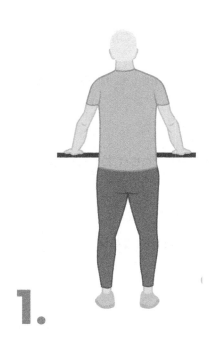

1.

2.

This exercise is similar to back leg raises; it helps you build your thigh muscles. You can do this lying down, but for best results, it is best if you stand.

You will need something to hold onto for this exercise, so it is best to have a counter, chair, or walker with you when practicing side leg raises.

Instructions

1. Start by standing behind the object you are using to stabilize yourself. Keep your feet hip-width apart.

2. Lift your right leg to the side. Keep your posture straight and your body facing forward.

3. Repeat these two steps 15 times on each leg.

Variation: If you want to try a different way to raise your legs, you can try moving your legs forward and then backward. This exercise will help strengthen the muscles and joints in your legs, ankles, and feet.

EXERCISE 10
WOOD CHOP

1.

2.

With this exercise, you will be able to work multiple muscles simultaneously in one simple movement.

The wood chop allows you to work the muscles of the shoulders, hips and trunk, as well as numerous abdominal and back muscles, improving balance and posture.

All you need is any heavy object. If you don't have a dumbbell, any object weighing between 1 and 5 pounds is fine.

Instructions

1. Start by standing with your feet hip-width apart. Grip the weight with both hands at the side of your right hip so that your body is slightly bent to the right.

2. Pivoting on the right foot, lift and rotate the dumbbell to the left side of the head

3. Pivoting now on the left foot, now bring the weight back from the left side of the head to the right hip.

4. Repeat the exercise 10 times on each side.

Tips:

- Keep your trunk as straight and stable as possible during the exercise.
- If you feel slight pain, slow down the speed of the exercise and decrease the weight. If the pain is more acute, stop performing immediately.

It is recommended to start with a lighter weight and adjust it based on the first 10 repetitions.

EXERCISE 11
MINI LUNGES

1.

2.

This exercise strengthens your legs to prevent the risk of falls. Lunges help with balance control because they enable you to brace and catch yourself before you fall.

1. Stand as straight as you can, with your feet shoulder-width apart facing forward. If you need to, hold onto something to maintain your balance.

2. Step your left leg directly behind you, keeping it straight.

3. Bend your right knee slightly. Make sure your bent knee is in line with your toes, not in front of them.

4. Hold the position for 15 seconds.

5. Stand back up straight and repeat with your other leg.

6. Do 3 repetitions for each leg for the best benefits.

Tips: When practicing mini lunges, it is important to know the risks. Make sure you don't lunge too far forward or backward, which can move your ankles in the wrong direction, or keep your legs too close together. If you have had knee surgery in the past, it is best if you skip this exercise altogether.

EXERCISE 12
MODIFIED CHAIR PLANKS

Planks are one of the best exercises you can do to support the loss of balance. They help you gain mobility and flexibility in your muscles, bones, and overall body. As a senior, however, doing a plank can be difficult, which is why we recommend a modified chair plank. It has the same benefits and steps but is easier on your body.

Instructions

1. Place your chair against a wall, and place your hand on the edge of the chair. Step both of your feet behind you.
2. Make sure both of your arms are straight, and your hips are aligned with your heels and shoulders.
3. Hold the position of the plank for up to a minute
4. Stand up straight in the starting spot.

Tips:

The plank is an exercise that can be quite difficult at first. Do not overdo it and listen to your body. If the first few days of training one minute of plank is too hard, try staying in position for 20 seconds. Then 30 seconds. Then 45 seconds.

You will see that with time the progress will be incredible!

EXERCISE 13
2-WAY HIP KICK

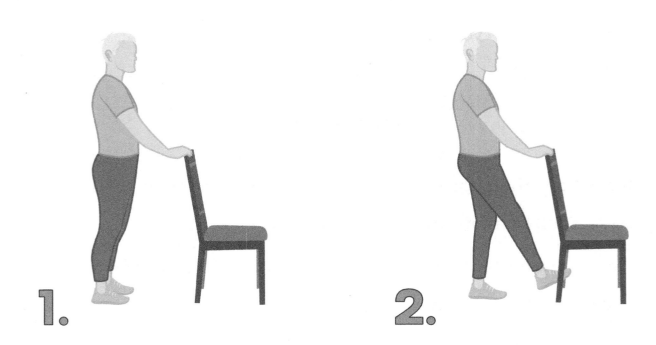

1.

2.

3.

This is a good exercise to build strength in your hips, which can help with stability when you walk and go up or down the stairs.

If you need to, you can use a counter or chair to support your balance.

Instructions

1. Stand, ensuring your feet are hip-width apart. Hold onto the counter if you need to.

2. Extend your left right fully in front of you, then bring your right back to the starting position.

3. Extend the same leg to your side, then bring your leg back to the starting position again.

4. Repeat these steps with the opposite leg.

5. Do this exercise on each leg 10 times.

EXERCISE 14
SIT TO STAND

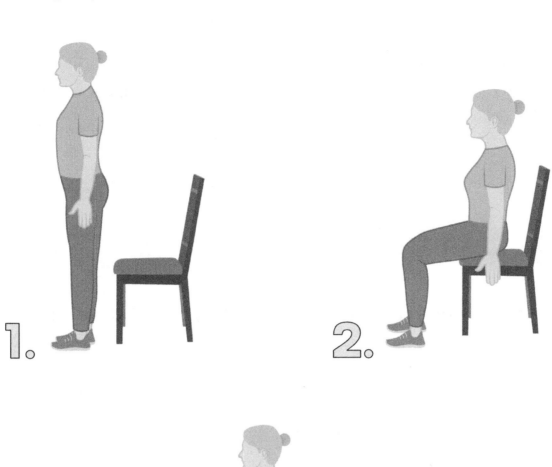

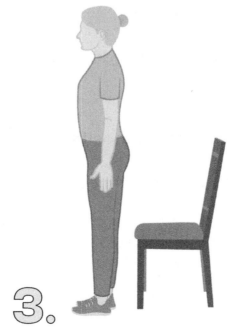

1.

2.

3.

As the name suggests, this exercise entails moving from a sitting to a standing position. You may need something to hold on to for support, although the goal of the exercise is to not use your hands if possible. Sit-to-stands help you regain and maintain your mobility, balance and posture.

Instructions

1. Stand straight up in front of a chair and bend your legs.

2. Sit down on the chair and pause.

3. Stand up again and pause.

4. Focus on using the muscles in your core and legs to rise and sit.

5. Repeat these steps 10 times then take a short break or move on to a new exercise.

EXERCISE 15
HEEL RAISES

This exercise is easy to do and doesn't require much movement, but it strengthens your lower-body muscles and can help you feel motivated and energized throughout the day.

Instructions

1. Stand up with your feet shoulder-width apart close to a counter or the back of a chair.

2. Elevate both heels off of the ground, putting all of your weight on toes, and balance there. Use your toes to grip and engage your core muscles to stay put. Keep this position for 2 seconds.

3. Keep your whole body straight as you are practicing these steps. When you feel comfortable enough, you can let go of the counter.

4. Repeat 20 times.

EXERCISE 16
MODIFIED BURPEES

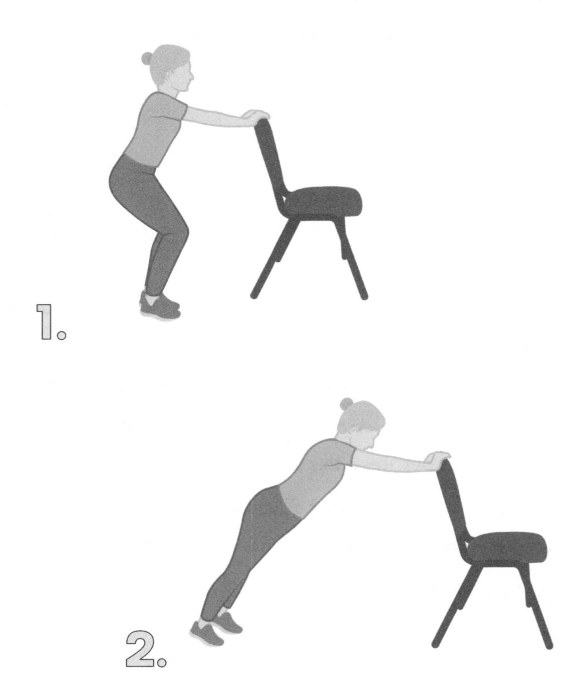

1.

2.

Burpees may sound like a digestive issue, but they are in fact an exercise! The modified version is easier for anyone who struggles with mobility. They help you gain muscle control and strength to combat challenges from vertigo.

Instructions

1. Grab a chair and place it against a wall with the back of the chair closest to you.

2. Stand up straight in front of the chair and align your feet with your shoulders.

3. Bend your knees, so you are squatting. Place both hands on the back of the chair. Keep your arms extended fully, making sure they are aligned with your shoulders.

4. Step one foot behind one another so you are slowly walking the lower half of your body outwards from the chair. Your body should form a line from your head to your heels, similar to a plank position.

5. Next, step one foot in front of the other to slowly move back into the starting squat position.

6. Stand up straight from the squat position.

7. Repeat this process 10 times to gain maximum benefits.

EXERCISE 17
2-POINT STANCE

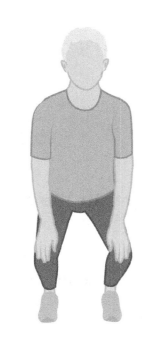

1.

2.

This exercise is known in the American football world—most players will do this before and after games, as well as during practices. The best part about this exercise is that anyone can do it, whether you are a teenager, adult, or senior. The 2-point stance exercise helps you become more flexible and improves your range of motion. It also helps you strengthen your lower body and back muscles and is very useful for increasing your sense of stability and preventing falls.

Instructions

1. Stand with your feet flat on the ground and aligned with your shoulders.

2. Bend forward slightly and put your hands on your knees, making sure your knees are bent a bit as well.

3. Keep your head up, looking into the distance.

4. Hold the position for 15 seconds up to 30 seconds.

5. Repeat this process 5 times, or as you feel necessary.

EXERCISE 18
SKATER SWITCH EXERCISE

1.

2.

This exercise builds muscle and bone strength. It also helps hips, legs, and glutes, while helping you control your balance and coordination. The skater switch exercise can keep your heart rate steady, which can improve cardiovascular diseases.

This exercise is super quick and easy; it's perfect for beginners. It involves no equipment and no hard work on your part.

Instructions

1. Stand and look straight ahead.

2. Bend your left knee slightly and bring your right leg back behind the left leg.

3. Bring your arms to the left side, then switch them to the right side, as you bring your right leg back to the starting position,

4. Switch legs and do the same thing.

5. Repeat this process 10 times to gain the maximum effects. It should feel as if you are skating in place.

EXERCISE 19
DYNAMIC BALANCE

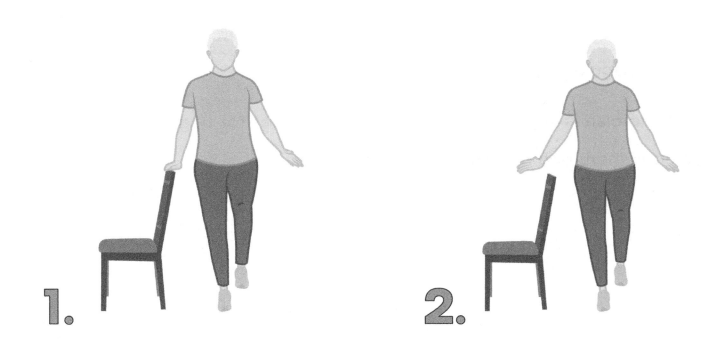

1.

2.

3.

This is one of the best balance exercises, as it allows us to practice balance in a dynamic, thus more realistic situation. You can practice this exercise daily to see pretty amazing results.

Place a chair to your right with the back facing you and use it for support.

Instructions

1. Start by standing with your feet hip-width apart and your hand resting on the back of the chair.

2. Slowly raise your left knee in front of you. Finding your balance, slowly lift your hand off the back of the chair, touching it only with your fingertips if necessary.

3. Now bring your leg slowly behind you, bending your knee slightly.

4. Continue repeating this movement by bringing your leg forward and back.

5. Repeat this exercise 10 times per leg.

Tips:

- If you are not comfortable taking your hand off the chair, you can always get more balance by touching the back with your fingertips only.

- Always keep your hand in close proximity to the back of the chair so that you have support in case you feel you might lose your balance while performing the exercise.

EXERCISE 20
SIDE LUNGES

1.

2.

This is a great exercise to improve balance and fall prevention skills while exercising lower body strength and flexibility. All you need is some side space and follow these simple steps.

Instructions

1. Begin the exercise by standing with your feet planted on the ground and your ankles in contact.

2. Move your right leg sideways, wide, bending your knee slightly, so that you shift your body weight to your right leg.

3. Now give yourself a push with your right foot so that you return to the starting position.

4. Repeat the previous step with your left leg.

5. Repeat the exercise 10 times per leg.

PART

2

SITTING BALANCE

EXERCISES

EXERCISE 1
ANKLE MOVEMENTS

1.

2.

Moving your ankles in certain motions is beneficial for improved joint mobility and motor control, and decreased risk of falling and injuries.

Instructions

1. Sit in a chair, making sure your back is flat against the back of the chair.

2. Lift one foot slightly off the floor and flex your toes, bringing them up towards your shin.

3. Point your foot forward, curl your toes, then straighten them out.

4. Repeat this process on your other foot.

5. Do 10 repetitions on each ankle.

Tips:

This is also a good exercise to practice as a warm-up or a cool-down, as it stretches out your ankles and leg muscles before or after exercising. When practicing ankle exercises, you will want to learn about the six movements in your ankle to understand how your ankle moves and stays flexible. These six movements include: Plantarflexion (dropping or pointing your toes), dorsiflexion (flexing your foot or raising your toes toward your shin), eversion (rolling the sole of your foot outwards), inversion (rolling the sole of your foot inwards), medial (rotating your ankle inwards), and lateral (rotating your ankle outwards).

EXERCISE 2
SEATED HIP MARCHES

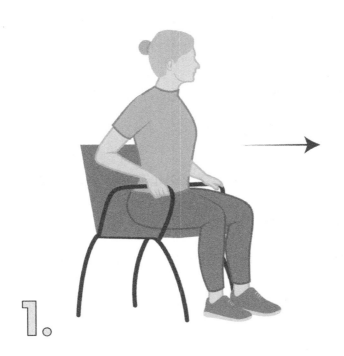

1.

2.

Hip marches are perfect to improve flexibility and mobility in your hips, particularly when you start to age. They build strength in your thighs, hips, and back.

Instructions

1. Sit on a chair with your back straight and your feet flat on the ground, a foot-length apart.

2. Hold onto the edge of the seat with both of your hands. Make sure to keep your back straight and tall in this process.

3. As you are still holding onto the chair, lift your right leg as high as possible, and keep the knee bent. Place your right foot back onto the ground, in the normal starting position.

4. Repeat these steps with your left leg. Perform 10 repetitions on each leg.

EXERCISE 3
ELBOW TO THE OPPOSITE KNEE

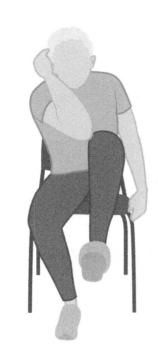

1.

2.

This exercise is very useful to train coordination and to strengthen the neuromuscular system, having more control of the body. Practicing this exercise daily, helps prevent the risk of falls and improve overall balance, reducing the risk of falls.

Instructions

1. Start by sitting in a chair, with your back straight and your feet flat on the ground.

2. Place your right hand behind the back of your head so that it forms a sharp angle with your arm.

3. From this position, raise your left knee and rotate your right elbow so that your right elbow touches your left knee.

4. Repeat the exercise 10 times.

5. Follow the previous steps, using your left elbow and right knee.

EXERCISE 4
BAND PULL-APART

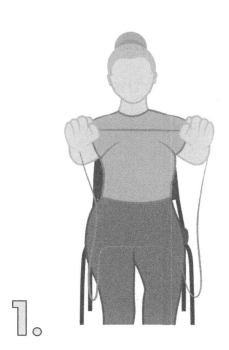

1.

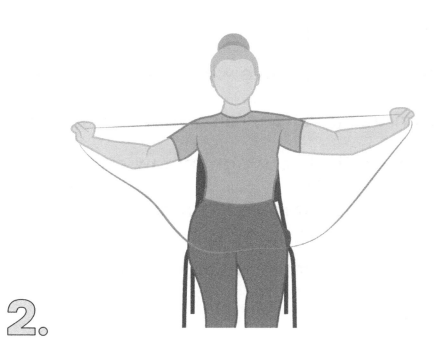

2.

This exercise helps you regain your balance by strengthening your arm muscles. It also helps to improve your posture and coordination.

When performing the band pull-apart, make sure you keep your breathing normal and your back muscles engaged, so you are using your core in addition to your arms.

In order to do this exercise, you will need a rubber resistance band.

Instructions

1. Grab a chair and sit on it.

2. Hold a mini resistance band in front of you with your arms outstretched and your elbows slightly bent. There should be no resistance in the band.

3. Pull your arms to each side, keeping them at shoulder height, so that your fists are moving away from each other. The band will stretch as your arms move outward.

4. Repeat these two steps 10 times.

EXERCISE 5
MODIFIED LEG LIFTS

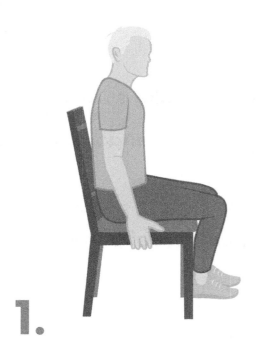

1.

2.

This is a great sitting exercise to do for balance as it builds strength in your abdomen and throughout your core. As a senior, it will help you become more stable when doing everyday tasks.

Instructions

1. Sit in a chair, with your knees and ankles touching each other. Ensure your head, shoulder, and spine are aligned so you don't strain your back or neck.

2. Grab the bottom of the chair. Keep your feet planted and knees together.

3. Exhale as you straighten your legs out in front of you, lifting your feet as high as you can.

4. Hold the positions for 5 seconds. Inhale as you lower your legs to the ground slowly.

5. Repeat this exercise 10 to 12 times.

EXERCISE 6
BALANCING WAND

1.

2.

This is a wonderful exercise to practice. It is performed seated in a chair, and you will need a cane or a stick of some sort to hold. This exercise works your balance and coordination, which reduces the risk of falling when you are at home or out.

Instructions

1. Hold the cane out in front of you in one hand while you are seated on the chair.

2. Open the palm of your hand so the cane lays flat on top and balance it there.

3. Keep your hand as steady as you can, and allow the stick to balance for as long as possible.

4. Switch hands every 30 to 60 seconds to practice balance on both sides of your body. Note any differences in your left and right sides.

5. Repeat the exercise 3 times per arm.

EXERCISE 7
SEATED JUMPING JACKS

1.

2.

Jumping jacks can be performed in a seated position to lessen the intensity of the exercise and the impact on your legs and back. Seated jumping jacks can help with your balance and coordination, as well as strengthen your arms and legs.

Instructions

1. Sit in your chair as straight as you can with your feet flat on the floor and your knees and ankles almost touching.

2. Swing your arms out to the sides and above your head, fully extended.

3. Move your bent legs out to the sides, as wide as you comfortably can.

4. Bring your arms down to your sides as you close your legs back together so your knees and ankles almost touch.

5. Do 10 full repetitions of seated jumping jacks.

EXERCISE 8
NECK STRETCHES

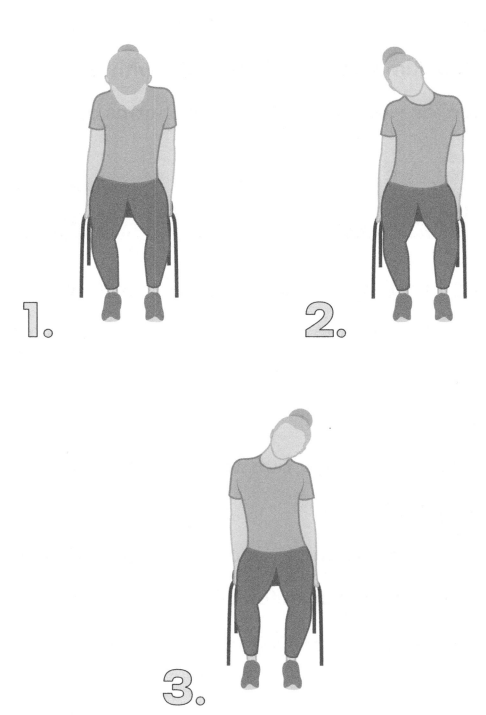

1.

2.

3.

As you grow older, your muscles and joints start to stiffen, especially around your neck, which can impede your range of motion. Stretching out your neck can relieve stiffness, pain, and inflammation in those areas, as well as regulate the crystals inside your inner ear. Neck stretches can take anywhere from a few seconds to a few minutes to do. Practice these stretches every day, and sometimes multiple times per day, for the best results—in the morning and at night, for example. Neck stretches are also a great way to warm up before tackling more strenuous workouts and to cool down after a workout.

Instructions

1. Sit tall with the crown of your head extended high.

2. Bend your head forward slowly. Hold the position for 30 seconds. Return to a neutral position.

3. Bend your head to the right so that your ear is parallel with your shoulder. Hold the position for 30 seconds and return to a neutral position.

4. Finally, bend your head to the left and hold the position for another 30 seconds.

EXERCISE 9
SINGLE LEG CALF RAISES

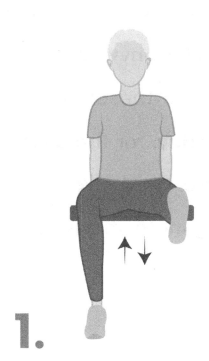

1.

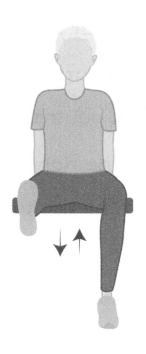

2.

This exercise strengthens the muscles in your calves, increases flexibility and mobility in your legs, and enhances your balance and coordination. When practicing calf raises, you will want to make sure that you do them slowly. For more of a challenge, you can use weights, such as dumbbells or ankle weights.

Instructions

1. Sit on a chair with your feet flat on the ground.

2. Slowly lift your leg straight out in front of you while keeping your foot flexed (toes pointed toward your shin). Hold for 5 seconds.

3. Slowly place your foot down on the ground and repeat the process with your other leg.

4. You'll want to stretch 10 times on each keg for the best benefits.

EXERCISE 10
REACHING

1.

2.

3.

This is a good exercise to control coordination and balance, as well as stretch out your back and body muscles.

Reaching is best when you have a partner to help you. There isn't a lot of movement involved, and only takes a couple of steps to follow.

Instructions

1. Have someone hold an object (e.g., a ball) in front of you. Fully extend your arms out in front of you. Reach as far as you can for the ball.

2. Make sure your partner is moving the ball to different positions (side-to-side and up-and-down), so you can stretch every muscle in your arms and torso.

3. Repeat this exercise 20 times.

EXERCISE 11
SEATED OVERHEAD STRETCH

1.

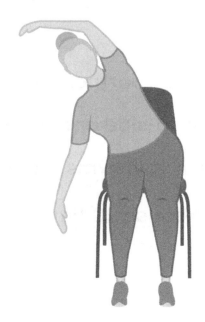

2.

This stretch can build strength in the chest, neck, arms, back, and shoulders. It helps to control your balance and improve your posture. Stretching also helps with mobility and flexibility in your body, both of which can start to decline as you age.

Instructions

1. Grab a chair and sit up straight. Place your feet on the ground so they are aligned with your shoulders.

2. Pull both of your arms over your head, making sure they are extended fully.

3. Lean to the right, bending at the torso until you feel a light pull on your left side. As you reach, be sure to reach *up* and out to the right.

4. Return your arms to their original overhead position and repeat step three, reaching your right arm *up* and over to your left side.

5. Do 10 repetitions with each arm, for a total of 20 arm movements.

EXERCISE 12
SEATED PEDALING

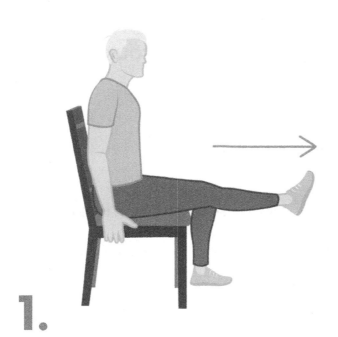

1.

2.

This is a great exercise to improve your balance and coordination. It also strengthens your quadriceps, calves, and hamstring muscles.

Instructions

1. Sit on a chair, with your back flat against the back of the chair. Place your feet flat on the ground and align them with your shoulders.

2. Lift your right foot up and then kick it out a bit, and bend your knee in a circular motion.

3. Repeat the circular motion with your left leg, just like you are pedaling a bike, one leg at a time.

4. Alternate legs at least 10 times for maximum benefit.

EXERCISE 13
GET UP AND TAKE A STEP

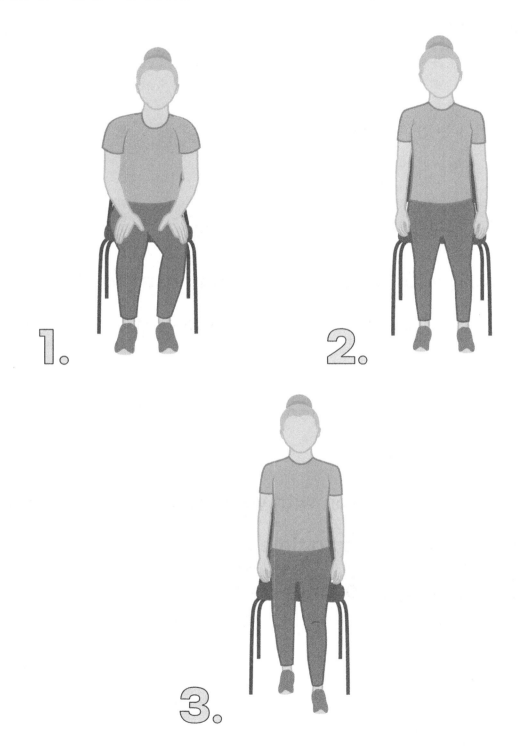

1.

2.

3.

This is a very simple exercise that is perfect for starting your exercise routine.

This exercise helps you increase your coordination and balance by replicating an action you perform every day.

Instructions

1. Start by sitting in a chair, with your feet firmly planted on the floor.

2. Helping yourself with your arms on your knees, stand up.

3. At this point, take a simple step forward with your right leg.

4. Bring your foot back and return to your seat.

5. Repeat this exercise 10 times, alternating which leg you step with.

EXERCISE 14
CHAIR RUNNING

1.

2.

This is the perfect exercise for seniors or people in general who suffer from balance issues. If you cannot go jogging, you can always try chair running—it has similar benefits, but you are seated the whole time. It can help strengthen your muscles, control your balance, and improve your coordination.

Instructions

1. Sit up straight in a chair. Let your arms fall to each side and make a light fist with each hand.

2. Bring your right knee up to your chest as you turn your left shoulder down to meet the right knee. In that same motion, bend your left arm at the elbow. Return to your starting position.

3. Bring the left knee up to meet the right shoulder and pump your right arm.

4. Repeat steps two and three in succession to create a "running" motion.

5. Each leg should be repeated 10 to 20 times for the best benefits.

PART

3

LYING DOWN BALANCE
EXERCISES

EXERCISE 1
FLOOR HAMSTRING STRETCHES

This exercise is particularly good to gain strength in your core, legs, arms, and hamstrings. It helps the hips stay in place, while increasing your mobility and flexibility to prevent falls.

Instructions

1. Lie down flat on your yoga mat or the floor. To start, bend your knees while keeping your feet flat on the ground.

2. Bring your feet off the floor with your knees bent. Wrap your arms around your legs.

3. Hold this position for 15 seconds.

4. Repeat this process 3 times per legs for maximum benefits.

EXERCISE 2
4-POINT KNEELING

This is a great exercise to increase the strength of your arms, legs, back and abs while improving your ability to balance and coordination.

Please note: If you find this version tricky, you can do the same exercise by lifting just the leg, without lifting the arm. This way you will have an extra point of support and the exercise will be easier.

Instructions

1. Kneel on the ground and place your palms to the ground, shoulder-width apart. Curl your toes under so your heels are pointed up to the ceiling.

2. Bring your left knee off the ground and raise your left leg backward (out and up)

3. At the same time, bring your right arm forward so that your left leg and right arm are aligned with your back. Hold the position for 5 seconds.

4. Repeat the same process raising your right leg and your left arm.

5. Repeat the process for 10 reps on each leg.

EXERCISE 3
MODIFIED CHAIR PLANKS

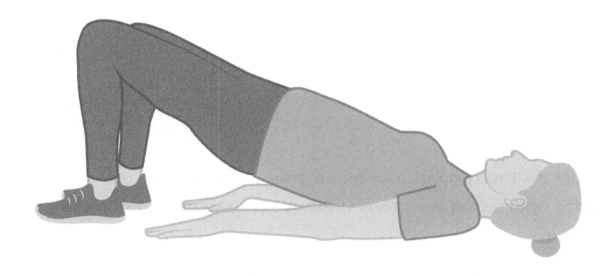

This is the perfect exercise to stretch out your back, legs, and chest and to strengthen your glutes and lower back.

The modified bridge is great for seniors, as it makes an otherwise challenging exercise much more attainable.

Instructions

1. Lie on your back on the ground, preferably with a yoga mat underneath for comfort.

2. Bend your knees and keep your feet flat on the ground, toes pointed straight ahead.

3. Lift your glutes slightly, so your back is fully off the ground, but your shoulders remain pressed into the mat.

4. Hold the position for 30 for best effects. You can make this stretch more advanced by elevating your feet and straightening your legs.

Tips:

When practicing any bridge stretches, there are some common mistakes to avoid. Raising your hips too high can lead to overextending your back, which may cause pain or inflammation. Lowering your hips too much can also cause undue strain. If you have recently had surgery, avoid this exercise as it may interrupt healing.

EXERCISE 4
ASSISTED KNEELING

1.

2.

This exercise will help you strengthen your knees, legs, arms, and stomach, as well as relieve pain and inflammation in your back. This exercise trains you to use your strength to keep your balance upright. It is especially good when you're experiencing dizziness, as you don't need to move much and it can reduce the symptoms you feel. Assisted kneeling exercises can also burn calories and fat and boost energy.

Instructions

1. Bend down and place one knee on the ground. You may need a pillow to protect your knee. Place your other leg in front of you for support with your knee bent at a 90-degree angle and your foot firmly planted on the floor.
2. Raise your arms to each side of your body, so you are in a "T" position.
3. Bring your head down slowly, so your chin is close to your chest.
4. Hold this position for 30 to 60 seconds.

Variations: There are many variations of the assisted kneeling exercise, and they all have the same benefits. Some are more complicated than others, but if you feel up for a challenge, you can practice them.

- Assisted kneeling with equipment: Use dumbbells and bring your arms out to the side, back down, then out in front of you.
- Tall kneeling: Place both knees on the ground and repeat the original exercise bringing your arms from a T position to both arms raised above your head.

EXERCISE 5
COMFORTABLE RECLINED TWIST

This is one of the best exercises you can do to improve your posture and strengthen those muscles that help prevent falls.

This version, suitable for older adults, is used to massage the hips and back and stretch and relax the spine. It is also a great exercise for lightly exercising the abdominal muscles.

Instructions

1. Lay down on a mat with your back pressed to the ground and your knees bent. Place your feet firmly on the floor with your toes pointed forward.

2. Let your knees fall slowly to the floor on your right side, keeping both of your shoulders pressed to the floor. You should feel a stretch in your left glute and lower back.

3. Bring your bent legs back to the starting position and drop the lower half of your body to your left side.

4. Repeat this process eight times on each side of your body.

Tips:

- Do this exercise three times a day.
- If you start to experience any pain, slowly finish your movement, then immediately stop.
- Whenever you do this exercise, you should increase it by one repetition. For example, if you do eight repetitions the first time, the next time you practice it, do nine.
- Make sure you are breathing normally while practicing supine exercises.

EXERCISE 6
SUPERMAN

1.

2.

You may not become a superhero with this exercise, but you will certainly improve your overall muscle structure, with significant benefits in posture, balance and fall prevention.

In fact, the superman not only strengthens the core, but also:

- The erector spinae muscles, providing support to the spine.
- The back muscles, helping to maintain correct posture and avoid kyphosis.
- The leg and glutes muscles, providing the lower body with more support to prevent accidental falls.
- The muscles of the lower back, so as to strengthen one of the most sensitive parts in terms of injuries, especially during physical activity.

Instructions

1. Lie on your stomach on a mat, with your legs extended and arms stretched forward.

2. Slowly lift your arms and legs about 5 inches off the floor until you feel a slight pressure in your lower back.

3. While contracting your glutes and abs, imagine that you are lifting your belly button slightly off the ground, as if you were flying (this is why the exercise is called superman).

4. Stay in this position for 2 seconds, maintaining regular breathing.

5. Return to the starting position.

6. Repeat this exercise 10 times.

EXERCISE 7
HEEL SLIDES

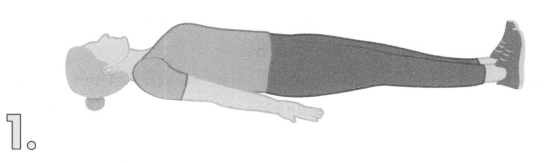

1.

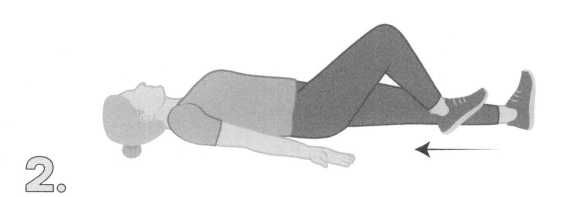

2.

Heel slides build strength in your ankles, legs, and knees. They increase the range of motion in your knees, so this exercise is especially beneficial when recovering from knee injuries or surgery.

Instructions

1. Lie down on your back on a mat on the floor or the bed. Keep your legs flat and straight.

2. Slide your right heel towards your glutes while bending your knee. If you can reach, grab your ankle with your hand and gently pull your heel back to increase the stretch.

3. Release your ankle and slide your heel back to the starting position, and then slowly lay your leg flat on the bed or floor.

4. Repeat with your left heel.

5. Do 10 repetitions, alternating legs as you go.

Tips: When practicing heel slides, keep these tips in mind so you don't injure yourself:

- As you pull your ankle back, be sure not to overextend the knee. Make sure you are comfortable. This exercise should not be painful.
- Before and after practicing this exercise, give your knee a massage. A good way to do this is with lotion or essential oils.
- Practice this exercise slowly. Don't go too fast or try to rush the process.
- If you are on a bed, place a plastic bag under your heel to be able to slide easily. If you are on the floor, wear socks or place a towel underneath your heel.
- Make sure your back is flat on the ground or bed.

PART

4

WALKING BALANCE
EXERCISES

EXERCISE 1
TIGHTROPE WALK

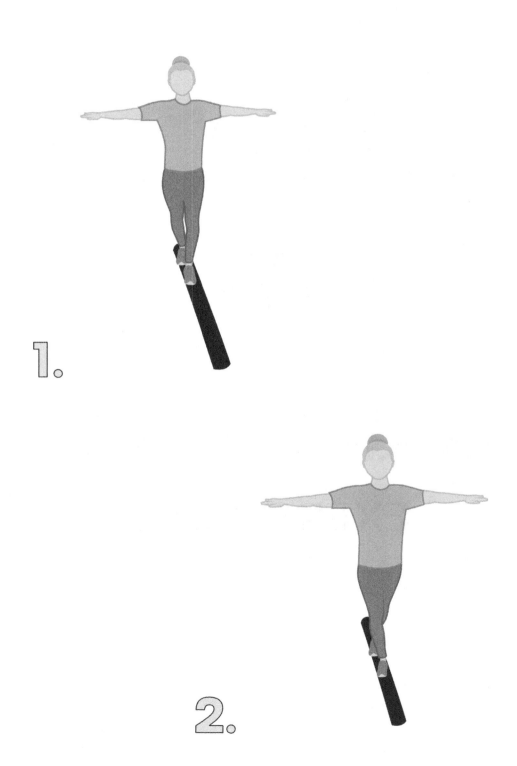

1.

2.

Walking is one of the best forms of exercise. The tightrope walk helps control balance and coordination while walking.

Instructions

1. Stand up straight and raise your arms out to your sides and bow your head to look at your feet.

2. Walk slowly and deliberately forward in a straight line by placing your right leg in front of your left and then switching legs.

3. Walk as far as you possibly can without falling over. Walk within arm's distance to a wall for support if you need to check your balance along the way.

4. You can also tape a line on your floor to make it easier to tell where and how you are walking.

EXERCISE 2
GRAPEVINE

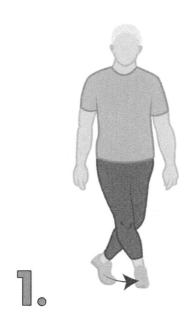

1.

2.

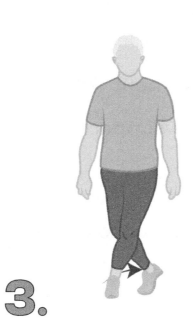

3.

4.

In order to control your balance with grapevine, you need to follow a few simple steps. Make sure you are using something to hold yourself up if needed

Instructions

1. Stand with your feet hip-width apart. Keep your arms down at your sides.

2. Cross your right leg in *front* of your left one and step down.

3. Step out to the left with your left leg so you are again standing with your legs hip-width apart.

4. Cross your right leg *behind* your left leg. Step out with your left leg so you are again standing with your legs hip-width apart.

5. By repeating steps 3 and 4, you can move across the room sideways in this manner.

6. Repeat these steps and move from one side of the room to the other.

EXERCISE 3
JOGGING IN PLACE

Jogging in place can be safer than running outdoors. You can remain in the comfort of your own temperature-controlled home, use furniture for support if you need to, and take rests whenever you feel necessary. Jogging has many benefits, including burning calories, helping you lose weight, improving energy and mood, and providing you with better balance and hand-eye coordination.

Performing this exercise is fairly self-explanatory, and you can do it at your own pace. All you have to do is stand in place and lift your knees one at a time and pump your arms.

Tips:

Before you jog, reach out to your doctor to make sure this is an exercise you can safely do. Jogging in place can cause pain in your shins, ankles, and hips if you do it too much or too often. Start slowly, take lots of breaks, and drink water before, during, and after you jog.

EXERCISE 4
HEEL-TOE WALKING

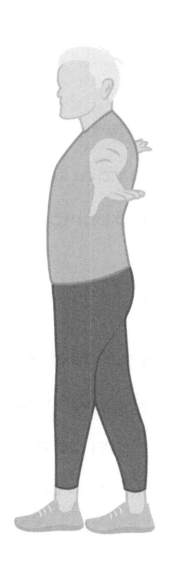

This is a great exercise to do if you experience balance issues. It is similar to the tightrope walk, but has different benefits, such as strengthening your legs and ankles, as well as your calf muscles.

Clear an area of your floor of tripping hazards before starting this exercise. To perform this exercise, there are a few simple steps to follow.

Instructions

1. Stand tall with your feet flat on the ground. Bring both of your arms out to the side and extend them.

2. Keep your head up and your eyes focused straight ahead. If you need to, use your peripheral vision to see the floor and things around you.

3. Place one foot in front of the other. Every time you step onto the ground, make sure you place your heel down first and then roll onto the balls of your foot and off your toes.

4. Walk 20 deliberate steps per leg.

10,000 STEPS-A-DAY CHALLENGE

This challenge is similar to the two-mile walk, but you are counting steps rather than distance. Anyone can do it; it just takes dedication and consistency. Walking daily improves your overall physical and mental health.

There are no hard and fast rules when it comes to walking. Be sure to get a tracker to follow your progress—this will help you achieve your goal. Tracking your walking progress can motivate you to maintain a proper routine to reach your goals. There are a few variations you can do while walking and tracking steps. You can choose how you want to proceed when walking.

- Go for a walk around your neighborhood.
- Go for a walk in nature.
- Walk around your house while doing daily tasks.

Tips:

You may need to start with 5,000 steps at first. That's perfectly fine because you don't want to injure yourself. Listen to your body.

EXERCISE 6
SIDE STEPPING

1.

2.

3.

4.

This is the perfect balance exercise for anyone who suffers from dizziness and nausea. It keeps your heart rate up and your blood pressure elevated. While there are some benefits to side stepping, you should also be aware of a few risks. You can hurt your knees, legs, ankles, and feet if you do this exercise at a fast pace and if your posture is not straight. You can also risk lower back pain. Go slow and be careful.

Instructions

1. Stand up straight with your feet together and bend your knees slightly.

2. Step to the right side with your right foot. Then take your left foot, and bring it, so it is touching your right.

3. Repeat this ten times per side. Feel free to go at a faster or slower pace, depending on your level of comfort. Bend your knees a bit deeper as you side step for more of a challenge.

Variations: There are a few variations to this exercise—some are simple, and some are more complicated. Remember, these are presented to give you options to mix up your routine.

- Banded side step: Tie a resistance band around your ankles so that when you step out to each side, you feel resistance.
- Side shuffle with ground touches: Instead of stepping out to a side, slide your foot along the floor out to the side and then tap your toes. Slide that leg back in and repeat on your other leg.
- Side step up: When you step to the side, step onto a low platform (a short step stool, a low step) and push up to a standing position. Repeat this several times on one leg and then turn around to work the other leg.

EXERCISE 7
MARCHING

1.

2.

This exercise is particularly great for seniors, as it reduces pain, inflammation, and any tension around the joints in your legs, knees, feet, and ankles. It strengthens your heart and improves your blood pressure and blood sugar levels. Practice this exercise no more than once or twice a week at most to prevent injury.

Instructions

1. Stand up straight, near a wall if you need some support.

2. Lift your left leg towards your chest, and bend your knee. Keep your back straight throughout this exercise.

3. Place your left leg onto the ground slowly and repeat the process with your right leg.

4. Do 20 repetitions on each leg.

Tips:
If you want to provide yourself with a challenge, you can always do these exercises slower—this will give you more control of your balance, and help you achieve good health overall. Remember, speed is not the goal with balance exercises.

EXERCISE 8
WALKING BY TURNING YOUR HEAD

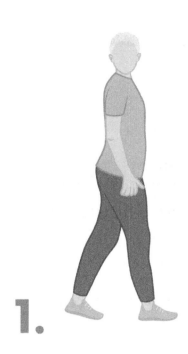

1.

2.

This is a great exercise that allows you to replicate an everyday life situation in a protected environment, such as your home. For example, think about the case you have to cross the street looking left and right. This is a frequent scenario that may seem trivial, but it is one of the classic situations in which you can lose your balance as an elderly person.

This exercise also helps improve neck flexibility and is great as a warm-up.

Instructions

1. Walk at a slow gait back and forth across the room.

2. As you walk, slowly turn your head first to the right, then to the center, and then to the left.

3. Keep repeating this movement as you are walking.

4. As you feel comfortable, you can slightly increase your pace.

EXERCISE 9
WALKING ON HEELS AND TOES

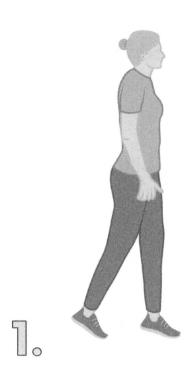

1.

2.

You can use this exercise at the beginning of your routine as a warm-up. It is a very simple exercise that you can practice either indoors or outdoors on a walk. Walking on your heels and toes is a great way to improve your agility, balance and strengthen your lower body.

Instructions

1. Start by walking normally back and forth across the room, being careful to keep your back straight and looking in front of you.

2. Now start walking on your toes for 15 seconds.

3. Now walk on your heels for 15 seconds.

4. Continue walking alternating between these 3 types of walking.

CHAPTER 6
30-Day 5-Minute-Plan for Balance Exercises

Understanding Workout Plans

The goal of a workout plan is to improve your balance, strength, and overall health. In addition, a workout plan is crucial to motivation, especially when you struggle with symptoms of balance loss because it can be hard to get up and do daily tasks, such as going to family gatherings or cleaning the house. When you have a plan in place, otherwise daunting tasks become doable. A plan helps you visualize what your future looks like and what you need to do to get there. Workout plans help you set realistic goals for your recovery and overall health.

Having a workout plan in place will challenge you to push yourself and at the same time, keep you safe from overdoing it and risking injury. When you create a workout plan, you have a guiding structure for your exercises. Everything is clearly spelled out—the length of the exercise, how many sets to do, what part of the body it strengthens, and how to practice the exercise efficiently. At the same time, you also have the flexibility to modify your workout whenever you want by introducing a modification to or variation of an existing exercise, or introducing new ones and discarding ones that aren't as beneficial. This keeps your workout routine fresh and exciting rather than boring and repetitive. You might decide to focus two days a week on sitting exercises and another two on standing or walking exercises. You might decide to alternate days working your lower body and your upper body—the options are endless.

It may take you some time to come up with a repeatable routine that works for you. Don't give up. The goal is to move. Some days exercise will make you feel incredible and you'll be extremely motivated. Other days may feel like an endless slog. That's perfectly normal for anyone in any age group—from top athletes to couch potatoes. The point of a workout plan is not to lock you in, but to provide enough structure to instruct and motivate you, while also providing enough flexibility to keep things fun and interesting.

The main thing, however, is to listen to your body and not overdo the exercises.

If you notice that an exercise is too strenuous, gives you pain or you feel dizzy, stop immediately.

Don't rush!

If you are patient the results will come and they will be amazing!

30-Day Plan

This 30-day workout plan is for people who are aging and want to regain their balance, independence, and confidence. It is designed to serve any fitness level, as the exercises are straightforward. Each workout will allow you to control your balance symptoms, improve your flexibility, and build strength in your muscles. These exercises will take you less than five minutes to complete and should be practiced daily for the greatest impact. Each exercise will benefit you in many ways—some will strengthen your legs, some will strengthen your core, and others will improve your overall balance. All of the exercises shared are designed for seniors and help reduce symptoms of balance loss.

This specific 30-day plan consists of four different exercise modalities: Standing exercises, sitting exercises, lying down exercises, and walking exercises. They are intentionally placed intermittently so that you don't do multiple standing exercises in a row.

The table will guide you to complete your workout plan as effectively as possible. Each column shows you what day you are on, which exercise to do, how much time it will take to complete, how many repetitions are required, and the recovery time in between each exercise.

The table tells you the name of exercise, the page on which to find the exercise, and the number of repetitions to perform.

Consider a recovery time of between 15 seconds and 30 seconds between exercises, depending on how you feel.

5-Minute Workout Plan

DAY 1

Tree Pose	Page 40	1 rep per foot
Sit-to-Stand	Page 60	10 reps
Elbow To Opposite Knee	Page 80	10 reps per leg
4-Point Kneeling	Page 108	10 reps per leg
Marching	Page 134	20 reps per leg

DAY 2

Comfortable Reclined Twist	Page 114	8 reps per side
Modified Leg Lifts	Page 84	12 reps
Foot Tap Steps	Page 48	10 reps – 3 times per leg
Weight Shift	Page 34	3 reps per leg

DAY 3

Side stepping	Page 132	10 reps per side
2-Way Hip Kick	Page 58	10 reps per leg
Flamingo stand	Page 42	3 reps per leg
Side Leg Raises	Page 50	15 reps per leg

DAY 4

Heel-Toe Walking	Page 128	20 steps per leg
Balancing Wand	Page 86	3 reps per arm
Sit-to-Stand	Page 60	10 reps
Modified Chair Planks	Page 56	1 rep

DAY 5

Heel Raises	Page 62	20 reps
2-Way Hip Kick	Page 58	10 reps per leg
Seated Hip Marches	Page 78	10 reps per leg
Seated Pedaling	Page 98	10 reps
Heel Slides	Page 118	10 reps per leg

DAY 6

REST DAY

DAY 7

Walking by turning your head	Page 136	1 minute
Get up and take a step	Page 100	1 rep
2-Way Hip Kick	Page 58	10 reps per leg
Back Leg Raises	Page 46	10 reps per leg

DAY 8

Walking on heels and toes	Page 138	1 rep per foot
Skater Switch Exercise	Page 68	10 reps
Seated Overhead Stretch	Page 96	10 reps per arm
Tree Pose	Page 40	1 rep per foot
Wall Push-Ups	Page 44	20 reps

DAY 9

Ankle Movements	Page 76	10 reps per foot
Foot Tap Steps	Page 48	10 reps – 3 times per leg
Mini Lunges	Page 54	3 reps per leg
Side Leg Raise	Page 50	15 reps per leg
Dynamic Balance	Page 70	10 reps per leg

DAY 10

Neck Stretches	Page 90	1 rep
Seated Overhead Stretch	Page 96	10 reps per arm
4-Point Kneeling	Page 108	10 reps per leg
Side Stepping	Page 132	10 reps per side
Sit-to-Stand	Page 60	20 reps

DAY 11

Chair Running	Page 102	10 reps per leg
Wood Chop	Page 52	10 reps per side
Knee Raising	Page 38	3 reps per side
Dynamic Balance	Page 70	10 reps per leg

DAY 12

REST DAY

DAY 13

Heel Raises	Page 62	20 reps
Side lunges	Page 72	10 reps per leg
Seated Jumping Jacks	Page 88	10 reps
Flamingo Stand	Page 42	1 rep per leg
. 2-Point Stance	Page 66	5 reps

DAY 14

Seated Hip Marches	Page 78	10 reps per leg
Sit-to-Stand	Page 60	10 reps
4-Point Kneeling	Page 108	10 reps per leg
Dynamic Balance	Page 70	10 reps per leg
Assisted Kneeling	Page 112	60 seconds

DAY 15

Jogging in Place	Page 126	1 rep per foot
Tree Pose	Page 40	2 reps per foot
Sit-to-Stands	Page 60	10 reps
Modified Leg Lifts	Page 84	10 reps per leg
Comfortable Reclined Twist	Page 114	8 reps per side

DAY 16

Side Stepping	Page 132	10 reps per side
Walking by turning your head	Page 136	1 minute
Modified Leg Lifts	Page 84	10 reps
2-Way Hip Kick	Page 58	10 reps per leg
Get up and take a step	Page 100	10 reps per leg

DAY 17

Heel Raises	Page 62	20 reps
Dynamic Balance	Page 70	10 reps per leg
Knee Raising	Page 38	3 reps per side
Superman	Page 117	10 reps

DAY 18

REST DAY

DAY 19

Seated Overhead Stretch	Page 96	10 reps per arm
Modified Leg Lifts	Page 84	12 reps
Skater Switch Exercise	Page 68	7 reps per leg
Modified Burpees	Page 64	10 reps
Knee Raising	Page 38	3 times per side

DAY 20

Walking on heels and toes	Page 138	1 minute and 30 seconds
Modified Bridge Stretch	Page 110	30 seconds
Flamingo Stand	Page 42	10 reps per leg
Get up and take a step	Page 100	10 reps

DAY 21

Elbow To The Opposite Knee	Page 80	10 reps
Seated Jumping Jacks	Page 88	10 reps
Walking by turning your head	Page 136	1 minute
Back Leg Raises	Page 46	10 reps per leg
Weight Shift	Page 34	3 reps per leg

DAY 22

2-Way Hip Kick	Page 58	10 reps per leg
Heel-Toe Walking	Page 128	20 steps per leg
Dynamic Balance	Page 70	10 reps per leg
Weight Shift	Page 34	3 reps per leg
Grapevine	Page 124	40 seconds

DAY 23

Seated Pedaling	Page 98	10 reps
Seated Jumping Jacks	Page 88	10 reps
Balancing Wand	Page 86	2 reps per arm
Side Stepping	Page 132	10 reps per side
Tightrope Walk	Page 122	60 seconds

DAY 24

REST DAY

DAY 25

Dynamic Balance	Page 70	10 reps per leg
Side Leg Raise	Page 50	15 reps per leg
Knee Raising	Page 38	2 reps per leg
Rock the Boat	Page 36	10 reps per leg
Assisted Kneeling	Page 112	50 seconds

DAY 26

Marching	Page 134	20 reps per leg
Floor Hamstring Stretches	Page 106	3 reps per leg
Side lunges	Page 72	10 reps per leg
Walking by turning your head	Page 136	1 minute
Heel Slides	Page 118	10 reps per leg

DAY 27

Get up and take a step	Page 100	10 reps per leg
Seated Hip Marches	Page 78	10 reps per leg
Weight Shift	Page 34	3 reps per side
4-Point Kneeling	Page 108	5 reps per leg

DAY 28

Floor Hamstring Stretches	Page 106	3 reps per leg
Seated Pedaling	Page 98	1 rep
Foot Tap Steps	Page 48	10 reps – 2 times per leg
Walking on heels and toes	Page 138	1 minute 30 seconds

DAY 29

Grapevine	Page 124	40 seconds
Balancing Wand	Page 86	3 reps per arm
Tree Pose	Page 40	1 rep per foot
Walking by turning your head	Page 136	1 minute

DAY 30

REST DAY

CONCLUSION

As you grow older, it is important to learn and understand your health issues and how to treat them. Doctors can help with a diagnosis and a treatment plan, but there are also home remedies you can practice, particularly when it comes to balance. Loss of balance is a daunting medical issue to experience and it can be extremely stressful for you and your loved ones. That's why it's very important to understand both the symptoms and causes. Just as crucial is knowing how to prevent falls. When you start to feel symptoms of dizziness, it may feel debilitating at first, but remember that you can take a proactive stance. There are several things you can do to alleviate symptoms and ensure your safety. These help a great deal when you aren't able to see a doctor immediately.

For starters, begin tracking when you start to feel symptoms, what they are, how long they last, how often they occur, and other related information. Take note of what and when you eat and how much water you drink as low blow sugar and dehydration can be contributing factors. You may start to notice patterns, which can be helpful when talking with doctors and preventing future symptoms.

Second, assess your living areas for potential hazards. Have an assistive device (cane or walker) handy to keep by your bedside, bathroom, and couch so that when you stand up, you have something nearby if needed. Use a handrail when walking up and down stairs to stabilize yourself. Wear comfortable clothing and flat shoes with rubber soles. Keep a flashlight by your bed and night lights on during the nighttime for when you need to walk around to prevent any falls or injuries from happening. Home safety is key when it comes to coping with balance issues.

Be sure to visit your doctor to better understand your situation and try several natural remedies, such as vitamins, herbs, oils, and certain foods and drinks.

Although natural remedies won't always cure balance problems, they can temporarily relieve symptoms such as dizziness and nausea, which can be miserable to live with for any length of time.

While it may seem counterintuitive, exercise is the most common way to relieve feelings of dizziness and nausea and ultimately guide you to a healthier and more relaxed lifestyle. To review, you can practice balance exercises by standing, sitting, lying down, or walking. Exercise not only helps with physical symptoms, but it can improve your mood and overall mental health too.

What can be tricky about exercise at any age is motivation. And as you grow older, your motivation can also decrease, which can make exercising regularly particularly challenging—even when you're getting results. That's why confronting motivation head-on is important. It helps to know yourself and what drives you. What might some of your goals be? What do you enjoy doing? Getting on the floor (and back up) to play with your grandkids, walking your local 9-hole golf course, getting your hands dirty in the garden again, completing that 5-K with your son or daughter, line dancing with your friends, hiking with your dog, reading without dizziness? Jot down a few of your goals in a journal. Make sure they are realistic and measurable so you can revisit them and assess how you're doing.

Now you can connect your goals to your workout routine so you can find ways to encourage yourself and remember what you're working towards. There are many ways to make working out more exciting. We talked about picking exercises you enjoy and trying out several variations so you can mix up your routine as you go. If you truly dislike an exercise, for example, it will be difficult to make yourself do it daily. Make sure the majority of the exercises you practice are fun and exciting to help you to stay motivated. You might also enjoy listening to your favorite upbeat music and singing along as you exercise. You can reward yourself with a healthy and delicious snack after a tough workout.

Accountability is another important factor in maintaining an exercise routine, which is why it's recommended to follow a workout routine and log your exercise over time. What can be even more helpful for many people is making exercise part of your social routine so that you are exercising with a friend or attending an exercise class at your local senior center, gym, or even online. Having people to exercise with can make it more fun and draw you back on days on which your motivation is low. Having the motivation to exercise is a skill to learn all on its own, and it does vary from individual to individual, but there are a few common tips to try to better organize your workout routine and provide you with the energy to exercise.

Fit exercise into your daily routine: Schedule a specific time in your day to practice exercises—this can be 30 minutes or less. If you don't have 30 minutes, try finding three 10-minute slots to work out. Remember, you can even work out as you are doing household chores, shopping, or even sitting on the couch. If you schedule your workouts and follow a plan, you will slowly create a habit, which will help you build motivation, strength, flexibility, and mobility and experience fewer balance symptoms.

Join an exercise group: Having support on your exercise journey is so important, particularly for seniors. Groups can help you meet new people who may experience similar health issues, which can remind you you're not alone and give you ideas for how to cope. Groups led by a knowledgeable instructor can also help you learn how to practice your exercises with the proper technique and rigor for your body. In exercise support groups, you can share tips, express opinions, and cheer each other on. In sum, groups can help you gain a more positive outlook on yourself, your health, and your life.

Make your workout routines fun and exciting: Exercises can be downright boring, especially if you continue to practice the same ones every day. But working out doesn't *have* to be boring! You can play music while you work out, or go to the gym instead of staying home. Mix your exercise routine up so you aren't doing the exact same thing every day. Make sure when you make a plan, you practice the exercises that make you joyful. Include exercises you practice standing, sitting, lying down, and walking.

Write your workout routine down, so it is easy to follow: Write down a plan for your exercises. This will help you feel less overwhelmed and more motivated to get started and continue on your fitness journey. Writing down your goals can help you understand where you are now and where you want to be in the future. Putting pen to paper is a good way to improve your memory and put a plan in motion. Every day you can read your routine and know exactly what you need to do.

Keep a journal of your progress: It is important when planning your workouts that you also track your progress as you continue. Set goals for your workout plan that are realistic and achievable, and write these goals down in your journal. Make sure to include how you are feeling each day, if your balance gets better or worsens, and keep track of your daily diet and water intake. Keeping track of your workout can stimulate the brain to exercise and will help you gain momentum as you build a healthy lifestyle.

Exercise with friends as part of a social gathering: You may prefer exercising alone, but if you haven't tried exercising as part of a group, you might be surprised by how much you enjoy it. Phone a friend or grab your significant other and perform exercises together that can improve your fitness and balance. You can also invite some friends over and practice morning yoga or evening stretching workouts. You can incorporate social exercises into your daily routine, such as going for a short walk with neighbors or coworkers. Better yet, try a few different group exercise classes for seniors, such as yoga, dance, stretching, or tai chi.

Reward yourself after achieving your exercise goals: This is an important step (and one that is often overlooked) because rewards motivate us. Think about how you can treat yourself and practice self-care. You can reward yourself in small ways, such as getting your hair or nails done or getting a massage. If you don't want to leave your house, you can also reward yourself by getting food delivered, or watching a baseball game or a new movie.

Don't forget to have fun in the process—exercising can be enjoyable! Incorporate your own personality into each workout you do, be excited about what you can achieve, and switch it up from time to time. You will be grateful that you did! Loss of balance is hard to deal with from any age, especially as a senior, but just know that you can do this. You will reap the benefits and improve your balance when you create and follow through with a workout plan. You are loved, you are worthy, and you can apply healthy routines to your lifestyle to live life well!

Made in United States
North Haven, CT
30 June 2023

38402634R00089